INTERNATIONAL MANAGEMENT

BY

LOKE CHEE SHONG

aberdeen university
press services

Published by Aberdeen University Press Services.

Printed in the United States of America

ISBN: 978-0-6152-3542-4

This book is printed on 8" x 11", perfect binding, 60# cream interior paper, black and white interior ink, 100# white exterior paper, full-color exterior ink. Prices are subject to change.

Cover Title Designed by Aberdeen University Press Services.

International Management
First Edition
Loke Chee Shong

*This book is dedicated to
dear Shirley, Joshua and Joyce.
Both Dads and Mums, my sister and aunts and uncles,
cousins, nephews and nieces.
- Loke Chee Shong*

CONTENTS

General Bibliography

KENICHI OHMAE THE BORDERLESS WORLD
Power and Strategy in the Global Marketplace, 1990 Harper Collins

THE FIFTH DISCIPLINE
The Art & Practice of The Learning Organization, Peter M. Senge, 1990 Century Business

List of Figures

List of Tables

Exhibits

Text References

Integrity in Organizations

An Alternative Business Ethic Gordon Pearson 1999 McGraw-Hill

Research in Ethical Issues in Organizations Vol. 1 1999 Pava Primeaux

Current Issues in Business Ethics Peter W F Davies Professional Ethics Routledge

Global Marketing Management, A Strategic Perspective, Toyne Walters, Allyn and Bacon

International Organizations Principles and Issues, Bennett, Prentice Hall

International Business, Ball McCulloch, IRWIN

International Management, Beamish, Morrison, Rosenzweig, IRWIN

Multination Enterprises and The Global Economy, Dunning, ADDISON WESLEY

Cultures And Organizations, Geert Hofstede, McGraw Hill

Human Resource Management, Dessler, Prentice Hall

Corporate Kinetics, Michael Fradette And Steve Michaud, Simon & Schuster

Contemporary Strategy Analysis, Grant, Blackwell

The Internationalization of The Firm, Buckley & Ghauri, Thomson

The Borderless World, Kenichi Ohmae, Harper Collins

Appendixes   *139*

Preface

The first edition of International Management.

Living in this digital age with rapid ceaseless development of technologies, organizations no longer operate within the boundary of their homeland, in production of goods or integrated services.

Due to technologies advancement, apparently, it seems that the world had shrunk into what a popular word used by many a 'Global City', where business transactions are no more confined regionally. Riding on technological advancement, businesses conduct their communications and negotiations through the use of the world wide web and video conferencing all in instantaneous time.

Living presently in this era, my aim and motivation in writing this book is to enable and encourage both Administrators and Managers to equip themselves thoroughly with knowledge and skills to meet this new challenge. Managers need a holistic grasp of a Global view in order to do business across borders. They need to understand Governmental Relations, Political Risk, Ethics and Social Responsibilities. It is therefore imperative and essential to study this subject termed as International Management.

Global Managers need to know what Strategies to apply in an International Context, what are the Cross-cultural Management aspects and the Cultural Dimensions of International Management. They need to know the 'How' of Intercultural Communications and Understanding and 'How ' to conduct Intercultural Negotiations.

Global Managers need to know Human Resource Development and Planning Skills in the light of the Global Context. They need to develop Global Leadership mind set in a Global setting. They need to practice Interpersonal Skills to develop International Teams.

Hence, International Management is an essential subject to equip Global managers to manage across boundaries and cross-cultural settings. This Text is written for both students as well as practicing managers in different industries. It serves as useful material that will also benefit students who are studying in areas such as Political Science or International Relations.

Loke C.S. Jason.

Chapter One

International Management : A Global View

Today's international managers are increasingly challenged by the many instantaneous changes taking place in the global scene. These changes provide a complex business environment, though opportunities are abundant, however these are blended with risks. There is a need for skilled international managers to make effective business decisions in business contracts. There is also the need to develop good interpersonal-relations in the Host country and also societal obligations to conform to business ethics. Experienced managers thrive in the international context, intuitively understanding how to gain the cooperation of their foreign partners and workers.

Countries and their economies have become interdependent leading to the presence of a global market place. To function in this global market requires a global perspective. Percy Barnevik, Chief Executive Officer (CEO) of Asea Brown Boveri (ABB), estimates that his company needs 500 or so global managers (among 30,000 managers worldwide), people who are internationally minded, at the same time also comfortable with their nation of origin.

The terms "international" and "global" to an extent can be used interchangeably. But it is important to understand the difference that has developed in their meanings. An international perspective describes managers involved in interactions primarily between two countries and cultures both their home country culture and another culture. This has been an adequate model for much of the world's international business activity. But, globalization means transforming our international perspective to a global perspective.

The emergence of the term global manager means in the broadest sense, reorganizing the way one thinks as a manager and as a student of management. Once scholar summarize it as the necessity for an alteration of our mind set. Thinking globally means extending concepts and models from a one to one relationship (we to them) to holding multiple realities and relationships in mind. Simultaneously and then acting skillfully on this more complex reality. This shift would mean, that even if a manager has a regional responsibility for example, marketing for Central and South America, it is likely that this job will demand more than an understanding of Latin cultures and a capacity to speak Spanish and Portuguese. The same manager also may have to deal with research and development (R&D) labs in Japan; Europe, and North America to provide them with customer information and to get updates on emerging new products. Likewise, the regional marketing manager may have to discuss product problems with manufacturers in Southeast Asia late at night, North America time, and then send a facsimile about the potential solution to an alternative supplier in Eastern Europe.

Most of the requirements of a global manager were presented at a symposium organized by the Board of Governors of the American Society for Training and Development and been tabulated as "Executive Traits Now and in the Future".

The requirements are listed below

Now

All-knowing
Domestic Vision
Predicts future from past
Caring for individuals
Owns the vision
Uses power
Dictates goals and methods
Alone at the top
Values order
Monolingual
Inspires the trust of boards and shareholders

The Future

Leader as learner
Global Vision
Intuits the future
Caring for institutions and individuals
Facilitates vision of others
Uses power and facilitation
Specifies processes
Past of an executive team
Accepts paradox of order amidst chaos
Multicultural
Inspires the trust of owners, customers and employees

This list is not exhaustive though but it encompasses many of the particular skills required by global managers. Going through the whole range of literature dealing with global strategy, global marketing, global operations management, and global human resource management. The authors also identified a profile of effective global executives as someone who has the ability to:

Develop and use global strategic skills

Manage change and transition
Manage cultural diversity
Design and function in flexible organization structures
Work with others and in teams,
Communicate
Learn and transfer knowledge in an organization

The development of these skills is a lifelong process, and it is unlikely that a single executive will master all of them. A new global economy is emerging that is shaped and driven by money flows as well as by goods and services. It is characterized by volatile foreign exchange, government policies, resistance to standardized products, and changing economies of scale of flexible manufacturing technologies. The eventuality is a shift in the worldwide business structure that is forcing managers and corporations to adjust and to shed their parochial views.

Effective international management starts with a knowledge of key variables in the global economic environment. In any industry in any country, managers must have an overall knowledge of the wheres, whats, whys and hows of the countries and regions of the world. This knowledge starts with the size and growth rates of country markets; their populations; their trade volumes, compositions, and growth rates; their natural resource bases and labour costs, and their financial positions.

This knowledge can be used by corporations as a first cut to identify the threats and opportunities that might arise in their international operations. It will assist these multi-national corporations to identify countries and regions to which they might export, from which they might import, and in which they might invest in manufacturing operations and factories.

We may be living in the "information age", but many a times we are ignorant to these basic facts like which countries have the highest income (Gross national product) per person in the world? Which are the 10 most populous countries in the world? Which countries have the largest markets? Which countries with populations over 5 million grew the fastest over the past 10 years? Which countries have the largest volumes of international trade? Which countries have had the highest growth rates in their trade volumes over the past decade? Which countries are among the top 10 as sources for foreign direct investment? As host countries?

Current data on population, GNP, purchasing power parity, and international trade statistics response to some of these questions. However, accompanying these data are also problems and inherent limitations, nevertheless, these data are still used by international managers to address some of the basic issues and decisions of international management.

International competitiveness has now evolved to a level of sophistication that many term as globalism. Global competition characterized by networks that bind countries, institutions, and people in an interdependent global economy. This global economic integration, had resulted in the growth rate of world trade rising faster than that of world gross domestic product. In other words, the trade of goods among countries has been increasing faster than the actual world production of goods.

As another indicator of globalism (reported in the 1991 World Investment Report issued by the United Nations), foreign direct investment in the 1980's grew more than three times faster than the world output of goods, reaching $196 billion in a year in 1989, concentrated primarily in the developed economies. The European Community (EC) has now caught up with the United States to share the position of the World's largest investor, but Japan is closing in quickly.

The United States has become the largest recipient of foreign direct investments, mostly from the EC and Japan, taking in almost half the world annual investment since 1983.

As for world corporate leadership, as of June 1992 the United States had regained ground from Japan from previous years, basically as a result of soaring stock prices in the United States and falling stock prices in Japan. Of the 100 largest corporations in 1992, 49 are American, compared with 42 in 1991 and 39 in 1990; 23 are Japanese, down from 37 in 1991 and 42 in 1990. However Japan still dominates in the banking industry, with seven of the top ten banks. In the overall, the Royal Dutch/Shell Company (Netherlands/United Kingdom) has taken over the number one position from Nippon Telegraph and Telephone (Japan), which fell to number three.

The competitiveness of individual multi-national corporations is clearly related to national competitiveness, which involves domestic strength, international trade, government involvement, and many other factors. One recent survey (compiled jointly by the International Institute for Management Development (IMD) in Lausanne, Switzerland, and the World Economic Forum in Geneva) compared the competitive, environments of 34 countries. Interestingly, out of the ten listed as 'developing' countries, seven are in Eastern or Southeastern Asia, with the so-called four tigers; Singapore, Hong Kong, South Korea, and Taiwan, heading the list.

The International Business Environment

International organizations have been viewed, from one extreme, as the vanguard of an emerging world government and, from the other, as an exercise in futility in fostering cooperation among sovereign states. Neither of these extreme views does justice to the role of international organizations in the present age. In this new millennium, the state, possessing the ultimate power and authority, remains the primary political unit. But, it is change, accommodation, and a proliferation of interstate and transnational contacts the hallmarks of an increasingly interdependent world.

This state system displays no signal of rapid deterioration or changing into new forms states however are reluctant to sacrifice their sovereignty to supranational entities. But humans are rational and capable of effecting adjustment or alternations to the system. Change is not only a major phenomenon of the modern world but it is occurring at an accelerating rate. Many changes have already taken place that must be considered in analyzing the relations of nations.

The Post-World War II world is enormously differentiated from the world of the 1930s. The spectrum of changing conditions is manifested by the rise of superpower armed with super-weapons; the collapse of the old colonial empires; and the focus of attention upon new problems of economic development, over-population, the environment, the advancement in space technology and the control of ocean resources. The ending of the Cold War shifted the international political focus to severe outbreaks of violence in places such as Somalia, Kuwait, and Yugoslavia, and the need to supervise transitions to new political regimes in such countries as Namiba, Nicaragua, and Cambodia. Another change is the rapid development in this new millennium, of an elaborate structure of international organizations, private and public, universal and regional, multi-purpose and specialized.

As the dusk of the twentieth century exits, competition is a popular global phenomenon, however this development takes place through gradual change rather than abrupt revolution. Though there were varying historic effects on trade of economic developments throughout the world, but during the last half a century, trade patterns had revealed a more definite profile of multinational expansions. Nevertheless, global commerce has increase in recent years, and more change is absolutely taking place more rapidly than at any other time frame in the face of history.

These changes, however, had affected different companies and countries of varying ways. Wealthy companies with huge resources definitely have found the best opportunities for efficient redevelopment of their assets, and global organizations often take opportunity to choose the best and advantageous markets to compete in. Firms engaged into multi-domestic industries, often encounter more difficulty in repositioning their assets and reorganizing foreign operations. Likewise, wealthy nations with established physical and capital infrastructures offer the most attractive markets for international expansion and most favorable positions for foreign direct investments. The dis-equilibrium in world's economies, encapsulated the less develop and the newly developing nations, some of these nations work through difficult transitions, from repressive ideological systems to free-market economies. Some may be bypassed by world events.

Within this framework, companies of many nationalities are growing into international markets. Some firms are simply exporting, while others are investing in foreign facilities, and global organizations creating companies of integrated technologies resulting in world-brand goods, services, and multi-cultural systems of management. With such variable categories of international business in the world, indeed no single word could described adequately what characterizes and constitutes international management of businesses. Individual firms choose to expand in many ways, and they employ a wide variety of strategies.

Social and Economic Changes

Global, trade has grown over the past two decades at an annual average rate of 8.4 percent, with a projection of 11.8 percent in the year 2000. Whilst, the average annual rate of change for world GNP has barely embracing 0.9 percent. However, in real terms, more than two-thirds of the world's increased economic activity in the past two decades had occurred through trade, and while some countries do experience domestic growth, there are many in economic decline and stagnation growth.

Status quo or deteriorating economies are in less-developed countries (LDCs) which are barren in social and economic infrastructures, which is capable of supporting sustained economic development. On the contrary, looking at the Developing economies (DE's), they have demonstrated capabilities for positive growth supported by appropriate social and economic systems. There are some countries where political transitions or social unrest are affecting their economic growth, and in this case even high-income countries can suffer short-term economic reversals. Nevertheless, though growth statistics alone cannot categorically differentiate LDCs from DEs, but, distinctions can be drawn, while emphasize place in variations of growth potential and their relative attractiveness in inducing of international investments. Economic changes, therefore, have important implications for international managers; decisions about where to compete, how to position foreign investments, and the relative risk of foreign operations. Table 1.1 list selected indicators of world GNP and trade data that illustrate the basis for the distinctions.

These data shows several different growth patterns. Firstly, the rate of per capital GNP growth for the high-income economies has more than doubled the world average since 1980, and the per-capita GNP growth rate for the low-income economies (including China and India) has more than tripled the world rate for the similar time frame. It is noticeable that without China and India, the low-income group's remaining economies have suffered a substantial net loss (-1.0 percent on the average). Likewise the middle-income nations went through a net loss too. Put differently, the affluent nation have grasped wealth whilst the poor nations have systematically lost economic ground, thus increasing the polarization in the world income distribution. The table does not show that China has achieved the highest average rate of per capita GNP among the world's low-income societies at 7-8 percent, India has averaged 2.9 percent in the similar time frame. Because of their huge populations, these two countries skewed the data and obscured the true picture of downside growth in economies such as Rwanda, Aserbaijan, Armenia, Nicaragua, the Congo, and twenty others.

The highest growth rates occurred among nations and territories that were considered underdeveloped until recently. These nations include Hong Kong, Taiwan, south Korea, Singapore, Thailand, Indonesia and Malaysia. Quite unexpectedly Thailand achieved the highest annual per capita growth rate of all nations at 8.9 percent. Notably but somewhere lower growth rates took place in Mexico, Jamaica, the Philippines, Sir Lanka, Ireland and Portugal. Clearly, nearly all high-income economies and a majority of middle-income economies enjoyed upside growth, however they rarely managed results very different from the world average. Approximately all of the world's heavy economic growth occurred in the countries of Asia. For example, Hong Kong and Singapore have attained placing among the world's most affluent economies; while others, remain in the middle-income and low-income groupings.

International managers find many more interesting trends in the trade data of Table 1-1. Firstly, the exception of the high-income group economies, the rest of the world experienced a tremendous increase in both exports and imports over the past 15 years, and the rate of change in both exports and imports for that time frame 1990 to 1995 almost doubled the 10 year rate during the 1980s time frame. World Bank research shows that China had experienced both the highest rate of change in exports (an annual increase of 14.7 percent) and the highest rate of change in imports (24.6 percent). Poland recently record a 3.9 percent increase in exports and a 26.5 percent increase in imports to parallel Eastern Europe, based on data for activity that take place in 1995 and 3 prior years. In retrospect, the rapidly growing Asian nations noted from table also proceed through double-digit expansion in both exports and imports, most low-income group nations with downside GNP growth suffered declines in trade. There are some exceptions, however, with economies in transition (the Baltic States, Eastern European countries, and a number of Latin American countries), these States, though trade increased but their GNPs remained status quo, even worst some downside due to domestic problems.

Table 1.1

Selected Indicators By Region For World Economies

	GNP per capita (weighted average)		Exports and Imports, Annual Percentage Change (weighted average in 1987 dollars)			
Regional Economies (Number of regions/ territories)	Dollars 1994	Percentage 1980-1995	Exports 1980-1989	Exports 1990-1995	Imports 1980-1989	Imports 1990-1995
Low-income (51)	$380	3.4%	5.7%	9.1%	1.6%	13.0%
Low-income (45) (excludes China and India)	360	-1.1	1.0	2.6	-4.0	3.9
Middle-income (57)	2,520	-0.1	3.5	7.0	1.0	9.8
High-income (25)	23,420	1.9	5.0	5.1	6.1	4.6
World total (133)	4,470	0.9	4.8	5.7	5.0	5.7

The GNP is US dollars normalized for exchange rates, and GNP percentage change is weighted average based on population.

Regional Trading Blocs – The Triad

Global Trade today is inclining toward a system of three regions free-trade blocs (Western Europe, Asia and North America) called the TRIAD market, they grouped around three dominant currencies, the deutsche mark, the yen and the dollar.

One researcher summarizes the impact of this new order influencing our perception of national boundaries as follows:

Today, if you look closely at the World TRIAD companies inhabit, national borders have effectively disappeared and, along with them, the economic logic that made them useful lines of demarcation in the first place.

Western Europe

In Western Europe, the famous cry of the common market countries had been the 'EC 92' which referred to the ultimate finalized agreement in 1992 among the twelve nations of the European community (EC) – Belgium, Britain, Denmark, France, Germany, Greece, Ireland, Italy, Luxembourg, Netherlands, Portugal and Spain. This agreement would create an internal market in which trade among these twelve member nations and their approximate 30 million people would be as free as trade among the United States. Since this goal was set, however, difficulties in gaining agreement to the MaaStricht Treaty, a plan for complete economic and political unity by 1999 have led to modifications in the agreement to gain cooperation among number nations and also to encourage potential new members.

Another recent pact will incorporate seven other neighboring Western European countries (Austria, inland, Iceland, Sweden, Norway, Switzerland, and Liechtenstein), members to the European Free Trade Association (EFTA) into the integrated market. Both organizations, however, remain separate distinct entities. This pact, will create the largest and most integrated common market in the world, namely the European Economic Area, with a population of approximately 376 million or more consumers as surveyed, stretching from the Arctic to the Mediterranean in a geographic area 50 percent more than the original EC market size.

EC '92 referred to the elimination of internal tariffs and customs, as well as financial and commercial barriers, effective January 1, 1993. Many problems still had to be resolved, however, issues such as cultural diversity, localized regulations and national standards, pricing differentials, tax rates, exchange rates and employment laws.

In dealing with the EC, international managers face two major tasks. One is strategic, how to deal with various possible results of the EC agreements, such as what has been called a 'Fortress Europe', that is, a market closed to outsiders. The other task is cultural, how to deal effectively with multiple sets of national cultures, traditions, and customs within Europe, such as differing attitudes, example, how much time should be spent on work versus leisure activities.

Asia

Asia's growing power represents a major corporate challenge to all outsiders, both in terms of withstanding Asia's global competitiveness and in terms of gaining access to Asia's growing consumer markets. With the consideration of the recently Asia crisis in perspective though, still the Pacific Rim economies, by the end of the last century and the beginning of this millennium, are expected to be bigger, in total, than those of the EC and about equal to those of North America.

Japan and the Four Tigers, the newly industrializing economies (NIEs) of Singapore, Hong Kong, Taiwan, and South Korea, each of which has unique factors of production, provide most of the capital and human resource expertise for Asia's developing countries. Economists observed a growing integration of the region, with Japan as a catalyst and a dominant but welcome partner as it replaces America as an investor. The dominating presence of Japanese investors had led some economic analysts to suggest that they may be laying the ground work for a regional economic bloc.

Certainly, the recent developments seem to lead to the believe of such an eventuality. In October 1991, the protracted war in Cambodia ended; North and South Korea agreed to an agenda for talks to end the 40 years of hostility between them, and the United States agreed to start talks toward regaining diplomatic relations with Vietnam. One astute commentator predicts that an Asia economic bloc would have a profound impact on the political and economic landscape of the twenty-first century's.

Asia's map is quietly realigning just as significantly as Europe's. The difference is that, while Europe and North America struggle with economic hard times, Asia is preparing for its next economic leap, fueled by trade, investment, and technology links among the Asians themselves, not withstanding the recent crisis. Asia is seeing the dawn of the Pacific Century.

The Japanese astute management practices and techniques that brought about their competitive success is noteworthy of commendation. The Japanese focus on long-term growth, and their willingness to postpone consumption to achieve that goal, rather than focusing, as Americans do, on short-term, bottom-line profit maximization for shareholders, accounts for much of their 'economic miracle'. Many researches show that Japanese factories, whether in Japan or in the United States, are the world's most productive. In several of their U.S. plants, the Japanese management employ nonunion workers, resulting in a $10 per hour advantage over American manufacturers. A business writer in Fortune notes that Japanese competition is so stiff that Detroit now sells nearly half of its compact cars at a loss.

Much of Asian's economic power and competitive edge comes from Japan's keiretsu and South Korea's chaebol. Both of them are large conglomerates of financially linked groups of companies that play a significant role in their countries; economies. Japanese Keiretsus, Mitsubishi and Toyota, to name two of the most powerful are regarded in Washington as forms of trade barriers they do business among themselves. Whenever possible, adding to the huge bilateral trade imbalance between the United States and Japan. Korea's chaebols, Daewoo, Samsung, Hyundai, and so on earn billions of dollars of revenue each year.

North America

In the North America, the extension of the free-trade agreement between the United States and Canada to include Mexico, encompass an area that stretches from the Yukon to the Yucaton is being commented as a move that will bring faster growth, more jobs, better working conditions and a cleaner environment for all as a result of increased exports and trade. This trading bloc, 'One America' consist of approximately 360 million consumers and generate about $6 trillion in total annual output, resulting in the Northern Hemisphere the largest market in the World, and one with that will expand into countries like Chile, Brazil and Argentina, as trade liberalization among the Latin American countries progresses.

The potential investment opportunities resulting form the North American Free-Trade Agreement (NAFTA), foreign companies have invested $80 billion in Mexico since 1988, with the value of U.S. direct investment in Mexico as of 1991 standing at $7.1 billion (although as compared to Canada at $66.9 billion is considerably less). With this union, American companies are setting up new manufacturing facilities in Mexico or extending their manufacturing and assembly operations in the mar

quiladeras, U.S. manufacturing facilities that operates just south of the Mexican-American border since the 1960s under special tax concessions.

Many Mexican and American organizations are also setting up joint ventures, such as the one between Wal-mart and Citra, the biggest retailers in the United States and Mexico respectively. The Mexican car industry is expected to double, perhaps even tripled, by this millennium. Already known as "Detroit South", the car industry south of the border is taking over more and more factory production for the Big three car makers in the United States, who are depending on the lower Mexican Wages (just $10 to $20 a day) and quality work to compete with Japanese are prices.

The Commonwealth of Independent States (CIS)

Mikhail Gorbachev's goal in the former Soviet Union was to privatize two-thirds of virtually all industry within a five year time frame in an attempt to use the capitalist system to salvage the soviet Union's failing economy. He named this program peretroika. This desperate attempt to move quickly from the crumbling centrally planned economy to a Western free-market economy did achieve some results though. Examples are Fiat offered to buy 30 percent stake of the VAZ auto works in Togliatti, local investors developed over three thousand commercial banks, and new private airlines were founded from the state carrier Aerofiat. However as the economy gradually improved, these limited initiatives did not work fast enough, to support the collapsing economy of the entire Soviet State structure, thus the subsequent formation of the Commonwealth o Independent States (composed of all but two republics that formerly made up the Soviet Union; Georgia and the Baltic States did not join the Commonwealth).

With all these recent, radical changes in the former Soviet Union, much of the region's economic future remains uncertain and unsettled. In fact, the former country now must be regarded as 15 separate States, or more.

Germany

Most investors await some even out of the chaos that has ensued in the reunified Germany. Even though a number of French, Dutch, and Austrian companies have already made deals, many foreign investors are still evaluating the eight thousand former Kombinats, or State holding companies, that operated in East Germany. These Kombinats are now being handled for restructuring, financing, and also sale negotiations by the treuhandanstalt (THA) trust company.

Other Regions in the World

The sweeping political, economic, and social changes around the world represent new challenges to international managers. The global move away from communism, toward capitalism, has had due influence on the world economy.

One of the most striking changes today is that almost all nations have suddenly begun to develop decentralized, free market systems in order to manage a global economy of intense competition, the complexity of high-tech industrialization, and a desire for freedom.

An area greatly affected by recent developments is the Eastern European bloc, where communism has proved unworkable, and collapsed. One significant result is the emergence of a new economic hierarchy, establishing various Eastern-bloc countries as have and have-nots. For example, the monthly per capita income in Poland, the Czech and Slovak Federal Republic, and Hungary is now many times higher than that in Romania , Bulgaria and Albania.

Global attention is now focused on a new market forming in Eastern Europe of approximately 430 million people, accounting for about 15 percent of World Gross

National Product (GNP) as recorded in 1989. The fact that, Hungary, the Czech and Slovak Federal Republic and the former East Germany combined have a GNP greater than that of China. A huge new market with invitingly low wage rates offer potential investors a new, low cost manufacturing opportunity.

However many impediments may hamper business growth, because East European countries lack the capitalist structure and systems to reproduce Western management practices easily. One analyst, remark that "Market research is unfamiliar. The closest thing to a market survey that many East Europeans have experienced is a government interrogation." Some companies are not disturbed by these problems. For example, Pepsi Co, bottled 100 million cases of Pepsi at 60 East European plants in 1990, and Procter & Gamble sells as much Crest toothpaste in Russia as in Canada.

Information Technology And Technological advancement

An important theme of the New Growth model stresses the crucial role of technological innovation in both domestic growth and international development. With similar importance, the theory emphasizes private industry's pursuit of innovations as opportunities for wealth accumulation motivate individuals and companies to risk new ideas and business ventures. The model's core element, however, focuses on the process by which foreign trade and investment diffuse technology and creates an upward cycle of new income and productive capacity.

The aspect of this model is based on Adam Smith's work. The very same idea was a recurrent theme in Adam Smith's work more than two centuries ago, which attributed the wealth of nations in part to their comparative advantages in trade. This theoretical framework considered technology to encompass the combine factors of production that added value to commerce and generated profits. Smith also emphasized that comparative advantage would persist only until the technology was diffused through competitors' assimilation of knowledge.

Of all the developments propelling international business today, the one that is transforming the international manager's agenda more than any other is the rapid advances in information technology. The speed and accuracy of information transmission are changing the nature of the international manager's job by making geographic barriers less relevant. One observer comment :

The world is being restructured in an unusually rapid, precise way because historic forces are at work beyond the power of charismatic politicians or the astute planning of business executives. The biggest event of our time is that unprecedented advances in computerization, telecommunications, and other forms of information technology are relentlessly integrating the world into a unified whole.

Information can no longer be centrally or secretly controlled by governments, political, economic, market, and competitive information is available almost instantaneously to anyone around the world, granting informed and accurate decision making. Even cultural barriers are being gradually lowered by the role of information in educating societies about one another. Americans, for example, were gripped by the dramatic portrayal on television of the cultural differences in Saudi Arabia during the Persian Gulf War. Television coverage in particular by CNN has forever changed the reporting of news; what was once a distanced perspective on past events is now brought to us in real time.

The dynamite growth of information technology is both a cause and an effect of globalism. These technology allow managers around the world to hold video conferences and teleconferences with one another, facilitating instant consultation and decisions a possibility.

New Challenges That International Managers Face

Social, economic, and technological changes discussed so far only dwell on the surface of the developments in international business. There are more important forces at work to change the fundamental nature of international management, some of them working in concert with each other while others have detrimental and disruptive effects. The global TRIAD of trading blocs, as discussed earlier, strengthens affiliation within these regions, but it builds interregional trade competition on a scale never before experiences. However some critics of the Trade alliances suggest that they project a head-on economic warfare amongst regions. These critics also compare Japanese business strategists to wartime samurai, and some characterize German economic leadership as 'saber rattling'. Business negotiators and politicians define boundaries with language about "trade wars", and corporate chiefs talk of "establishing beachheads" on foreign land.

Central and Eastern Europe has its own problems. These countries emerged from the yoke of Soviet idealogy are driving hard to become free-market economies. They are keen on building modern states based on private enterprise, but these sudden and abrupt shifts to the embracing of principles of market economies risk various aspects of changes which arises from total change of mindsets and lifestyle of the people. These people were originally nurtured and moulded in a centrally planned economies and directed behavior cannot be overnight self-proclaimed and self-determined entrepreneurs. Furthermore these strong-willed people, though undeterred in their new found aspirations may lack the experienced to run and direct privatized businesses in an assumed overnight 'miracle' to take place.

The destruction of state-directed economies has only created a new found economic chaos, which these private enterprises will never be able to replace and bring back economic growth and stability in a short time period. Therefore this economic transition period will only harbor and breed unemployment, depression and deprivation, both sowing and reaping the seeds of social unrest. Government cannot mandate successful private enterprise in an overnight dream, anymore than its policies can ensure prosperity.

On the contrary, the circumstances in three of the world's five largest countries, namely China, India, and Indonesia are experiencing rapidly accelerating development. In fact, all of Southeast Asia is drastically changing with new international interests and vibrant trade economies. South America has quietly emerged on the international platform with exceptional progress among its leading nations. The Middle East remains troubled and much of Africa is either in transition or struggling, yet nations in these regions could determine and make a difference to international trade.

These global events, transitions, expansions and development implied an exponential increase in demand for qualified international mangers who can meet the challenges of a rapidly changing world. These international managers not only must be just knowledgeable in the head, but also cognitive to adapt themselves to other cultures and patterns of thinking and acting common among citizens in other nations. They must learn to work in diverse environments through interrelated networks of firms. This requirement implies association with many foreign interest struggling with their own priorities of growth and development.

Government Relations And Political Risk

Globalization and the explosive presence of multinational corporations projected a world where politics will be secondary to commercial inertia. To some degree, the governments should be proactive to accept subservient roles to global economic development, and politicians cannot ignore the importance of international business to their agenda on national development plans. In fact, both governments and politicians often find themselves caught up in the economies of transnational business.

Like multinational corporations, they must accept the challenges of forging global business relations. National agendas, home-country politics, and local economic development could not escape the dynamic influences of the borderless world of international commerce. Kenichi Ohmae (1) in his book, The Borderless World, 1990, talks about global citizens pages 18 to 21. On a political map, the boundaries between countries are as clear as ever. But, on a competitive map, a map showing the real flows of financial and industrial activity, those boundaries have largely disappear. He further quoted, that "Global citizenship" is no longer just a phrase in the Lexicon of futurologists. It is every bit as real and concrete as measurable changes in GNP or trade flows.

The same is happening for corporation. In the pharmaceutical industry, for example, the critical activities of drug discovery, screening, and testing are now virtually the same among the best companies everywhere in the world. Scientists can move from one laboratory to another and start working the next day with few problems. They will find equipment with which they are familiar, equipment they have used before, equipment that comes from the same manufacturers.

Drug industry is not the only example. Most people, for example, believed that it would be a very long time before Korean companies could produce state-of-the-art semiconductor chips things like 256k NIMOS DRAMAS. This is not so. They caught up with the rest of the Triad in only a few short years. In Japan, not that long ago, a common joke among the chip making fratenity had to do with the "Friday Express". Japanese Engineers working for different companies in Kyushu, Japan's south western "silicon Island", only 100 kilometers or so away from south Korea, would catch a late flight there on Friday evenings. Over the weekend they would work privately for south Korean semiconductor companies. This was illegal and violated the engineers' employment agreements in Japan. Nonetheless, so many took the flight that they had a tacit gentleman's agreement not to greet or openly recognize each other on the plane. Their trip would have made no sense, however, if semiconductor-related machines, methods, software, and work stations had not already become similar throughout the developed world.

Similarly you work into a capital goods factory anywhere in the developed world, and you will find the same welding machines, the same robots, the same machine tools. Likewise, all trading rooms for stocks, bonds, and currency look identical to the reuters and Telerates terminals; so much so that the traders switch companies quite liberally. When information flows with relative freedom, the old geographic barriers become irrelevant. Global needs lead to a global products. For international managers, this flow of information places a high premium on learning how to build the strategies and the organizations capable of meeting the requirements of a borderless world, or the ILE.

The disintegration of the Soviet State and subsequent reform movements in Central and Eastern Europe attest to the priorities of global economics over indigenous idealogies, but, ironically, government and political institutions have not become less important to world trade. In fact, politicians must accept a broader role in regional and global competition, orchestrate their own national interests with those of other nations, and protect their own economies against encroachment or deterioration.

Global integration does not release international managers from their concern for political and legal mandates; indeed, they must become far more sensitive to these factors. An organization must plan carefully where to allocate facilities, how to situate its operations, and extent of its exposure to risks that is inherent in international business.

In local decision making, international managers must comply with host-country laws, deal adapting with foreign regulations, and understand the political priorities of host governments. International managers also must comprehend the relationships between their companies' home-country governments and their host-country governments. For example, a U.S. corporation with business in China may feel threatened by a perceived human rights violations. These organization may maintain good trade relations in China, but gain little from the effort if home-country policy initiatives suddenly disrupt its activities. In these and many other situations, multinational corporations can be caught up in circumstances beyond their control. International managers often can do little to prevent the difficulties that they face, yet they must recognized these risks of doing business abroad in order to draw-up effective plans and conclude decisions.

Country Risks And Political Risks

Every multinational corporation has, by definition, chosen to operate in certain foreign countries. Perhaps the reason to go overseas has emerged coincidentally as part of trade transactions, or perhaps it represents a proactive action on the corporation venture. Whatever the reason for this decision, however, international managers should attempt to assess the risk involved. These risks associated with foreign investments and operations are named as either country risk or political risk. These two terms imply neither identical nor mutually exclusive meanings.

Country risk includes the uncertainty associated with government continuity, regional politics that affect the country, ineffective legal and regulatory systems, currency instability or obstacles to convertibility, and home-host country relations.

Figure 1-1

Country Risk and Political Risk

Country Risk	Political Risk
Macro issues of government continuity, Regional politics, legal and regulatory Systems, currency stability, home-host Country relations, trade alliances.	Macro and Micro issues associated with commercial interests, political decisions, social and cultural issues, and financial and economic risks.
Diplomatic Concerns Including Commercial Risk and Interests	Business Concerns for Asset Losses or Risk to Employees or Operations

Political risk is associated specifically with the commercial interests of companies involved in trade or international investments. It refers to the probability that political decisions, events, or conditions in a country including social conditions and trends, will affect the business environment in a way that exposes firms to financial or material losses.

Diplomats and business personnels look at many of the same variables when assessing country or political risks, but a multinational corporations should focus their concern on specific risks such as expropriation of its foreign assets, physical and intellectual security, trade restrictions, labor relations, procurement systems, licensing, cost of trade, and transactional difficulties such as constraints on profit repatriation and convertibility of currency.

A different way of understanding country risk identifies it primarily as a summation of macro issues, such as relationships between the home and host countries. The other components of country risk include international treaties, ideological differences, and host-country economic and social systems. Currently, new problems have surfaced, such as risks of terrorist activities. For example an American company doing business in China exposes itself to a far greater country risk than one doing business in Britain, because of ideological differences and tensions trade relations magnify uncertainty of operations in the Asian nation. Terrorism in both Colombia and Peru results in high country risk profiles for both nations.

Political risk also has a macro component, since a firm's relationship with the host government and differences in cultural values or social systems produce important influences on a firm's success. However, political risk is more often associated with micro considerations, such as specific trade restrictions, potential government interference with a subsidiary's operations, or particular regulatory constraints. For example, an American company in China faces a macro political risk due to unpredictable government policies as well as micro risks associated with China's inability to enforce intellectual property rights.

Country and political risk are influenced by host-country relations with other societies and by a firm's activities in other countries. For example, an American company with business interests in Israel may not be welcome in neighboring Arab States or vice versa. Again, in recent trade talks between the United States and China, the Chinese delegation threatened retaliatory sanctions against U.S. companies because Taiwan's president was allowed to visit the United States.

Management And Foreign Relations

Various events that influence country and political risk are beyond a firm's control. Other difficulties depend on relationships between its managers and representatives of the host-country government. Different patterns emerge in these relationships may imply relative differences in risk exposure, but every international business situations exposes a firm to some risk.

Situations become more complicated when a multinational corporation operates in many different countries, where some are potentially at odds with one another. Consequently, International managers must monitor relationships with a number of foreign constituents and keep themselves well informed about their own governments foreign relations. The differences in business systems that influence international management decisions will have tremendous impact on the firm's perspective and the management of their foreign relations with the host governments. International mangers have to recognize and establish a frame-work for understanding the risks associated with doing business abroad and be able to manage the relationships between host-government and organizational interests.

Political And Legal Systems

Ideological Forces

Such names as communism, socialism, capitalism, liberal, conservative, left wing, and right wing are used to describe governments, political parties, and people. These names indicate ideological beliefs.

Communism

Communism is Marx's theory of a classless society, developed by his successors into control of society by the communist party and the attempted worldwide spread of communism. In communist countries, the government owns all the major factors of production. With minor exceptions, all production in these countries is by State-owned factories and farms. Labor unions are government controlled.

Communism as conceived by Karl Marx was a theory of social change directed to the ideal of a classless society. As developed by Lewin and others, communism advocates the seizure of power by a conspiratorial political party, the maintenance of power by stern suppression of internal oppositions, and commitment to the ultimate goal of a worldwide communist state. Although private firms for non-communist countries usually cannot own plants in a communist country, they can do business with it. The recent developments in the People's Republic of China, the former Soviet Union , and Eastern Europe are opening opportunities for foreign investment.

Compensation for expropriated property

Until today, none of the communists governments has compensated the foreign former owners directly. However, a few of the owners have gotten some reimbursement indirectly out of Assets of the communist government seized abroad after the communist government confiscated foreign private property within its country. For example, the U.S. government sized assets of the Soviet Union in the United States after American property in the U.S.S.R. was confiscated. American firms for individuals whose property had been confiscated in the U.S.S.R. could file claims with a U.S government agency, and if they could substantiate their loss, a percentage of it was paid.

Expropriation and Confiscation

The rules of traditional international law recognize a country's right to expropriate the property of foreigners within its jurisdiction. But these rules require the country to compensate the foreign owners, and in the absence of compensation, expropriation becomes confiscation. Expropriation is government seizure of the property within its borders owned by foreigners, followed by prompt, adequate and effective compensation paid to the former owners. Confiscation is government seizure of the property within its borders owned by foreigners without payment to them.

The Collapse of Communism

A brief recollection of the reasons for communism's failure as an economic and social system is gathered. A couple of basic reasons would give some light to the collapse of communism.

The U.S.S.R. concentrated its best scientists, engineers, managers, and raw materials in production for the military; it neglected production for consumer goods. Gross production was the goal, the managers would go to ridiculous extremes to be able to report the production figures set by government central planners.

Since Soviet central planning allowed only one condom factory and birth control pills were very expensive under the communist regime, they were rarely available except to the privileged. As a result, abortion was by far the country's most common form of birth control. All these abortions were then counted as part of doctor's gross production and therefore swelled the reported national income.

Factories under construction got a certificate putting them into commission on the scheduled completion close even though they were almost never actually completed on schedule. Because of the certificate, the factory had to report production coming from it even though it had not yet produced anything.

Many enterprise uses many different deceptions, for instance, a factory reaching only 50 percent of its targeted output could have made a small change in its next shipped machine and doubled the price, from $10,000 to $20,000, thus doubled output.

Capitalism

Capitalism is an economic system in which the means of production and distribution are for the most part privately owned and operated for private profit. The capitalist, free enterprise ideal is that all the factors of production should be privately owned. Under ideal capitalism, government would be restricted to those functions that the private sector cannot perform, for example, national defense; police, fire, and other public services, and government to government international relations.

Reality in so-called capitalist countries is quite complex. The governments of such countries typically regulate privately owned businesses quite closely and frequently these governments own businesses.

Regulations and Screening

All businesses are subject to countless government laws, regulations, and screening in their activities in the United States and all other capitalist countries. Special government approval is required to practice the professions, such as law or medicine. Tailored sets of laws and regulations govern banking, insurance, transportation, and utilities. States and local governments require business licenses and impose use restrictions on buildings and areas.

Complying with all the laws and regulations and coping with screening require expertise, time, and of course, expenses. A business found in non-compliance may incur fines or even the imprisonment of its management.

Socialism

Socialism is public, collective ownership of the basic means of production and distribution, operating for use rather than for profit. Socialism advocates government ownership or control of the basic means of production, distribution, and exchange. Profit is not an aim.

In practice, so-called socialist governments have frequently performed in ways not consistent with the doctrine.

European Socialism

In Europe, socialist parties have been in power in several countries, including Great Britain, France, Spain, Greece, and Germany. In Britain, the labor party, as the socialists there call their political party has nationalized some basic industries, such as steel, ship building, coal mining, and the railroads, but has not gone much further in that direction. A vocal left wing of the labor party advocates nationalizing all major British business, banks, and insurance companies.

LDC Socialism

The less developed countries (LDCs) often profess and practice some degree of socialism. The government typically owns and controls most of the factors of production. Among the characteristics of an LDC are shortages of capital, technology, and skilled management and labor. Aid from DCs or from international organizations usually comes to (and it is hoped, through) the LDC government. Most of the educated citizens tend to be in or connected with the LDC government. It seems that the government would own or control major factories and farms.

If the LDC government is not communist, it will make occasional exceptions and permit capital investment. This happens when the LDC perceives advantages that would not be possible, without private capital. The advantages could be more jobs for its people, new technology, skilled managers or technicians, and export opportunities.

Risks for businesses dealing with Socialist Countries

There is an extremely wide range of practice among the countries that profess socialism. At the extreme, organizations must be careful to comply with all the applicable laws and regulations, as in any capitalist country. At the other extreme, such an LDC, where most or all of the major production factors are government owned, in international firm must do business much as it is done in a communist country.

Conservative or Liberal

Conservative is a person who wishes to minimize government activities and maximize private ownership and business. A right wing a more extreme conservative. Liberal in the 20th century United States, is a person who urges greater government involvement in most aspects of human activities. A left wing is a more extreme liberal.

We should not complete the subject of ideology without the mention of these words as they are common in used in the mid and late 20th century. Politically, in the United States, the word conservative connotes a person, group, or party that wishes to minimize government activity and to maximize the activities of private businesses and individuals. Conservative is used to mean something similar to right wing, but in the United States and the United Kingdom, the latter is more extreme. For instance, the conservative party, one of the major political parties in the United Kingdom, is said to have a right-wing minority.

There is at least one exception the generalization that conservatives wish to minimize government activities ; the anti-abortion movement calling for governmental control of abortion decisions. Although not all anti-abortionists are conservative, the press presents their position as such.

Politically, in the United States in the 20th century, the word liberal has come to mean the opposite of what it meant in the 19th century. It has come to connote a person, group, or party that urges greater government participation in the economy and regulation or ownership of business. Liberal and left wing are similar, but the latter generally indicates more extreme positions closer to socialism or communism.

Privatization

Privatization of government-owned and operated firms and services popularized through the 1980s; and by 1991, the selling of state assets from airlines to telephone companies had captivated politicians everywhere, even in Socialist Spain and Communist China.

Countries that privatization movement is prevalent are Canada, the United States, Mexico, Chile, Brazil, Britain, France, Spain, Italy, Holland, Germany, Turkey, Thailand, Singapore, Japan, the Philippines, Malaysia, Pakistan, and Argentina. Britain, during Mrs Margaret Thatcher, was the acknowledge leader of the movement. During her 11 years as prime minister, Mrs Thatcher decreased state-owned firms from a 10 percent of GNP to 3.9 percent. She sold over 30 firms, raising some Sterling Pounds 65 billion.

Private Sector More Efficient Than State

Proof beyond doubt may be impossible to achieve. Academics nonetheless pursue and attempt. However one study found that it cost the New York Department of Sanitation $40 (of which $32 was for labor) to deal with a ton of rubbish. It cost private collectors only $17 (of which $10 was for labor).

Research done in Australia's airline industry found that the private airline, Ansett, considerably more productive than the public sector's Trans Australian Airline. In survey interviews done by researchers, a large majority of managers moving from the public to the private system say that privatization has improved their performance. They reported the demoralizing effects of political interference and bureaucratic delay when their companies were government owned.

Other Forms of Privatization

Privatization may not always involve ownership transfer from government to private entities. For example, activities previously conducted by the State may be contracted out, as Indonesia has contracted a Swiss firm to operate its customs administration and Thailand has private firms operating some of the passenger line on its State-owned railroad. Governments may lease State-owned plants to private entities, as Togo has done, or they may combine a joint venture with a management contract with a private group to run a previously government-owned business, Rwanda did this with its match producing factory.

Global Trend

The global trend toward privatization, the sale of government-owned operations to private investors is spreading from Western to Eastern Europe and indeed to all corners of the world. This trend emerges as world competition escalates and the restraints of socialism are shunt in favor of free market enterprising.

The global trend toward capitalism and the attempts at privatization and deregulation to achieve a capitalist economy even in LDC's can be illustrated by recent developments in various South and Central American countries. In Mexico, the government has privatized some 750 enterprises, including the banking and telephone industries.

This kind of activity is similar in other Latin American countries. In Argentina, the movement is on to privatize state firms, everything from airlines to zoos is on the block. Argentina has already sold off its flag carrier, and its telephone company, and dozens of other assets, including utilities and railways, are up for grabs. Venezuela has sold two banks and is looking for buyers for its telephone company, airline, ports, and even a caracas race course. Brazil, after much delay, has announced plans to float 27 companies. Honduras is selling its Cheese factory,

Foreign firms are now welcome in South America as military regimes are shunt, and free-market economics is replacing floundering economic nationalism, state ownership, protectionism, monopolies, subsidies, and price controls as an avenue to increase economic growth.

This wave of capitalist sentiment has also spread to Asia. In Pakistan, the prime minister is attempting to move "like lightning" to deregulate Pakistan and establish a market system for its population of approximately 110 million people. The government themselves has begun selling off its 115 state enterprises (mostly un-profitable) and abolishing currency controls that have stamp out foreign investment.

Unfortunately, privatization is not as easy as it sounds. Whether in Pakistan or Argentina, the problems involved in selling state-owned firms, resulted in the havoc of inefficiency that have incurred colossal losses over the years are not easily deciphered.

Nationalism

Nationalism is a devotion to one's own nation, its political and economic interests or aspirations, and its social and cultural traditions. It has been called the "secular religion of our time". In most of the older countries, loyalty to one's country and pride in it were based on such shared common features as race, language, religion, or ideology. Most of the newer countries, in particular Africa, have accidental boundaries resulting from their colonial past, and within these countries, there are several tribes and languages. This has resulted in civil wars, as in Nigeria and Angola, but it has not inhibited these new countries from developing instant and fierce nationalism.

Nationalism is an emotion that can cloud or even prevent rational dealings with foreigners. The ills of a society can be blamed on foreign firms, which is what the chief of the joint staffs of the Peruvian military did when the military forces took charge in Peru.

Some of the effects of nationalism on International Firms are:-
1. Requirements for minimum local ownership or local product assembly or manufacture;
2. Reservation of certain industries for local firms;
3. Preference of local suppliers for government contracts;
4. Limitation on the number and types of foreign employees;
5. Protectionism, using tariffs, quotas, or other devices;
6. Seeking a "French solution" instead of a foreign takeover of a local firm; and
7. In the most extreme cases, expropriation or confiscation.

Why Firms Are Nationalized ?

The presupposition that government ownership of the factors of production is only to be found in communist or socialist countries, but this presupposition may not be correct. Because there are large segments of business owned by the governments of numerous countries that do not consider themselves either communist or socialist. From country to country, there are wide differences in the industries that are government owned and in the extent of government ownership.

There are a number of reasons, sometimes overlapping, why governments are involved with firms. Some of them are :-
1. To extract more money from the firms, the government suspects that the firms are concealing profits;
2. An extension of the initial reasons, is that the government believes it could run the firms more efficiently and make more money;
3. Ideological, when left-wing governments are elected, they sometimes nationalize industries, as has occurred in Britain, France, and Canada.
4. To obtain votes as politicians, save jobs by reviving dying industries on life support systems, which can be later disconnect after the election;
5. Because the government has placed money into a firm or an industry the control of the firm usually follow the larger shareholder; and
6. Happenstance, as with the nationalization after World War II of German owned firms in Europe.

All governments are in business to some degree, but not within the communist nations or LDCs. However, the government that had gone far into business are Italy and France.

Italy

The Italian government-owned Institute for Industrial Reconstruction (IRI) has been named as "the industrial octopus". In 1978, IRI was a leader in one category, it lost more money, an estimate of $980 million, compared to any other company. (The number two loser was another state-owned company, British Steel, which lost $793 million). The Italian government owns companies in many industries, namely, salt, tobacco, matches, mining, railways, airlines, auto manufacturing, steel, telephone, power plants, banking, restaurants, chocolate and ice cream making, radio and television stations, and refineries. IRI continues in the growth cycle and by 1991 it controlled 477 firms employing more than half a million people.

In the middle of 1980's, IRI established a new management that turned a majority of its companies around so that it reported a profit in 1990. Though its shipbuilding and airline businesses are still recovering very slowly.

British Steel being the second loser, having become privatized, by 1991 had become the World's most popular integrated steel firm.

United States

From historical records, the United States has been opposed to nationalizing industries, but it made an exception in that direction when it established the consolidated Rail Corporation (Conrail) in 1976. Conrail took over six bankrupt railroads in the northeastern United States. A decade later, the U.S. government was trying to sell Conrail; one proposal was to sell it to a private rail company, but this had evoked opposition form Conrail managers and employees as well as from competing railroads. Instead, its stocks was sold publicly to private buyers who included many Conrail workers and mangers. From then on, the United States has done very little to privatize government-owned businesses or operations.

France

The French government has been in business for centuries. When Louis XIV began building the magnificent Versailles Palace, the plans included thousands of mirrors and crystals chandeliers. The Venetians were the dominant glass makers of the World at that time, and Louis's finance minister, Colbert, did not want to pay them for all those mirrors and chandeliers. Colbert then set up the firm named as Saint-Gobain, and Louis insisted on owning the firm himself, rather than allowing idle nobles and courtiers own it. Louis feared that if they owned the company, they would become rich and powerful and potential rivals to his rule.

Similarly, Socialists did not nationalize the Renault automobile firm. Charles de Gaulle's post-World War II government did so to avenge its founders collaboration with the occupying Germans. Renault has drawn money from the French government for investments and has made occasional profits in the past years since then.

France's state-owned business account for almost one-third of the nation's GNP. State-owned manufacturers and banks employ about a million people thus contributing to both the GNP and employment.

In France, Britain and Italy, some government-owned firms have been brought into profitability. One distinct example is Usinor Sacilor. As late as 1986, the French company had the reputation of being one of "Europe's most intractable industrial and political nightmares". However in that year a professional manager with no political links was put in charge. He was able to make heavy industrial investment in modern, efficient equipment and to improve employee efficiency through training and better job flexibility. In 1988 Usinor Sacilor produced its first profit in 14 years, in 1989, it paid its first dividend in 15 years.

In 1991, the French government relaxed its prohibition against sale of government-owned company shares. This decision permits both domestic and foreign investors to take minority stakes up to 49.9 percent in state firms. Usinor Sacilor and a number of other firms and banks began negotiating for new capital and partners.

Unfair Competition ?

When government-owned firms compete with privately owned firms, the private firms sometimes complain that the government firms have unfair advantages. Some of these complaints are :-
1. Government owned firms can lower prices unfairly because they can afford to breakeven
2. They can obtain lower interest financing;
3. They can hold down wages with government assistance.
Another major advantage of state-owned firms over privately owned business comes in the forms of direct subsidies, payments by the governments to their firms. They total some 100 billion ECUs per year.

International Companies (ICs)

International business is not merely a passive victim of political force. It can be a powerful force in the World political arena.

The World's Top Economic Units Are Firms, Not Nations

An IC negotiating with a country may be bigger than the country. According to rankings in 1989, General Motors' sales of $127 billion made it the 20th largest economic unit. Its sales were larger than the $109.7 billion GNP of Finland. Ford's sales of $96.9 billion made it the 23rd largest economic unit, surpassing Norway. Of course, the GNP of the great majority of other countries is even smaller.

These financial size wields financial power. However, an IC's power need not rest solely on size. It can come from the possession of scarce capital, technology and management, plus the capability to deploy those resources around the world.

An IC may have the processing, productive, distributive and marketing abilities necessary for the successful exploitation of raw materials or for the manufacture, distributors, and marketing of certain products. These abilities are frequently not available in LDCs. Recognition of the desirability of IC investment is growing.

Country Risk Assessment (CRA)

Country risk assessment (CRA) is a bank or business having an asset in or payable from a foreign country, or considering a loan or an investment there, evaluates that country's economic situation and policies and its politics to determine how much risk exits of losing the asset or not being paid.

It is arbitrary and irrelevant to discuss this subject in this section on Government Relations and Political Risks, because country risk assessment (CRA) involves many risks other than political risks. As it is an important topic, sufficient to warrant a separate section.

Even though it is arbitrary to place CRA here, however it is not unreasonable since the political events of the last decade and until now had influence and caused firms to focus much more on the practice. Many firms that had already done CRA updated and strengthened the function, also many other firms began to practice CRA.

Types of Country Risks

Country risks are increasingly political in nature. There are wars, revolutions, and coups. Less dramatic, but nevertheless important for businesses, are government changes by election of a socialist or nationalist government, which may be hostile to private business and particularly to foreign-owned business may be hostile to private business and particularly to foreign-owned business.

These risks may be both economic or financial in nature. These may also be persistent balance-of-payments deficits or high inflation rates. The repayment of loans may be questionable.

Labor conditions may also cause investor to refrain and pause. Labor productivity may be low, or labor unions may be militant. Laws maybe changed on subjects such as taxes, currency convertibility, tariffs, quotas, or labor permits. The possibility for a fair trial in local courts requires assessment. Terrorism may be present. If it is, what options, can the firm protect its personnel and property ?

Information Content for CRA

The types of information a firm will need to judge country risk will vary according to the nature of its business and the length of time required for the investment, loan, or other involvement to yield a satisfactory return.

Nature of business

For example, the needs for a hotel company compared with those of heavy equipment manufacturers or manufacturers of personal hygiene products or mining companies. Banks have their own sets of problems and information needs. Sometimes there are variations between firms in the same industry or on a project-to-project basis. The nationality of the home country of the company may be a factor; does the host country bear a particular animus, or friendly attitude, toward the home country ?

Length of time required

Export financing usually involves the shortest period of risk exposure. Usually, payments are made in 180 days or less, and exporters can get insurance or bank protection. Bank loans can be short, medium, or long term. However, when the business includes host country assembly, mixing, manufacture, or extraction (oil or minerals), long-term commitments are necessary.

With long-term investment or loan commitments, there are inherent problems with risk analysis that cannot be resolved. Most of such investment opportunities require 5 to 10 or more years to pay off. But the utility of risk analyses of social, political, and economic factors decreases precipitously over longer time spans.

Who Does Country Risk Assess?

Various general or specific analyses, macro or micro analyses, and political, social and economic analyses have been conducted, probably under different objective names for the past. The conference Board located bits and pieces of CRA being performed in various firm's departments. For example, the international division and public affairs, finance, legal, economics, planning, and product-producing departments. Often the efforts are repetitive in nature because people in one department were unaware that others in the organization were also involved.

Efforts are attempted to concentrate CRA and to maximize its effectiveness for the firm. These efforts include guidelines on the participation of top management.

Another source of country risk analysis is the outside consulting and publishing firm. As CRA has emerged is perceived importance, numerous of such firms have been formed or have expanded.

Besides using the services of outside consultants, some firms in fact had buttressed their internal risk staffs by hiring such experts in the field of international business or political science professors or even retired state department, GA or military personnel.

CRA Procedures

The Economist Intelligence Unit breaks its assessments down into three categories. First, there is medium-term lending risk, covering such factors as external debt and trends in the current account. Second is political and policy risk, including factors such as the consistency of government policy and the quality of economic management. Third is short-term trade risk, including foreign exchange reserves.

The International Country Risk Guide (ICRG), established by a U.S. division of International Business Communications Ltd of London, takes a somewhat different approach. It offers individual ratings for political, financial, and economical risk, plus a composite rating. The political variable includes factors such as government corruption and how economic expectations diverge from reality. The ratings look at such things as the likelihood of losses from exchange controls and loan defaults. Economic ratings take into account such factors as inflation and debt service costs.

Lessons of the International Debt Crisis

There are at least five lessons that CRA analysts should be aware of and learned. First, many developing countries are vulnerable to external shocks. One important aspect is a country's export and import structure in weathering an external economic shock. For example, the newly industrialized countries of Asia with their diversified export structures have been in a much better position to deal with the collapse of commodity price and the erection of protectionist barriers than have been other countries with a comparable level of development but lopsided export structures (such as in Indonesia and Mexico).

Second, the development of debt crisis has clearly shows that the economic policies of debtor countries have a decisive impact on default risk. Those countries that have become most deeply mired in the crisis are the ones that adopted expansionary fiscal and monetary policies. The consequential results were inflation, current account deficits, loss of international competitiveness, and capital flight. Examples of such are the Philippines and the high-debt countries of Latin America. By contrast, those countries that allowed the altered world market prices and demand conditions to take effort on their economies and adapt their economic policies to accommodate changed conditions have fared much better than those that don't. Restrictive fiscal and monetary policies damped inflation, however occasional devaluation of their currencies kept trade balances under control. Example, the South Koreans withstood the debt crisis through skillful economic policies.

Third, sustained economic growth is a major requirement for high-debt countries to service their debts and reduce its burden. Austerity alone should not be the solution, economically, politically, or socially.

Fourth, the social and potential political costs of over-indebtedness combined with austerity neo league are proving high. In Latin America, real imports sell by about 30 percent, and real per capita income by some 7 percent, between 1981 and 1985. Social and political tensions had risen sharply and threaten the survival of several democratically elected governments. This in turn, greatly increases the danger of a debt moratorium

The fifth lesson from the debt crisis for CRA analysts is the global ripple effect of seemingly independent risks or economic shocks. For example, would be the oil price collapse at the beginning of 1986 jacked up oil-exporting countries' default risk while lessening that risk for oil importers thus affecting international interest and exchange rates and triggering a whole series of fiscal and monetary policy reactions.

The 1987 stock market crash caused worldwide economic reverberations other events that would have global affects if they were to occur include sustained changes in world interest rates, recession on major market countries, creation of debtor-country cartels, or the banking system's loss of confidence in the whole region.

Business-Government Relations

International management organizations and international managers should prepare to cope with potential problems, such as detrimental policies or political uncertainties inherent in "rule of mass" situations. Such foreign circumstance, require a frame of reference for understanding how a multinational firm will manage its foreign assets. There are various business-government relations models that could be applied to specific aspects of political risk that a firm can face in its foreign operations.

A Framework for Business-Government Relations

Most international managers gauge political risk according to subjective measures of the likelihood of a mishap perhaps a miscommunication in trade relations or in the operations of a foreign subsidiary as a result of host-country political, economic, or social circumstances. The framework for understanding business-government relationships is vital prior to the application of formal methods of assessing risks. Such framework must reflect the risks associated with four sets of relationships.

Table 1-2

Business and Government Relationships – Four View Points

Relations between	Concerns of International Managers
Host government and company	Political instability, currency convertibility Government intervention or expropriation, Regulation, security, property rights export/imports Controls, taxes, etc.
Home government and company	Home-imposed sanctions, treaty constraints, Domestic laws applicable overseas, export/import licenses, taxation, currency restrictions, etc.
Home government and host Government	Ideological differences that strain relations, embargoes, boycotts, trade treaties, sanctions, licensing, home or host pressure on business to achieve political ends.
Host government and other Government	Secondary influences on relations between host and third countries, regional treaties or trade restrictions, re-exporting sensitive products, ideological pressures etc.

Host Government and Organizational Relations

When an International manager considers political risk, they implicitly contemplate about business in a particular country and relationships with the host government. These relationships may include government investment in the organization, government support or incentives for the multinational business or contractual obligations with the government contracts to a certain extent, often specify local procurement of government owned materials or resources. Host governments usually use favorable import/export agreements to attract organization to locate within their borders, and they often negotiate reductions in customs duties or grant favorable tax rates. These relationships also include regulatory control of foreign subsidiaries and legal constraints on their operations, but the most difficult concerns of multinationals focus on the potential for government to impose politically motivated trade sanctions.

As new political leaders come to power in a host government, nationalism may lead them to apply sanctions, and economic conditions may lead them to establish protectionist measures. These moves may seem almost arbitrary, and politicians in every country may apply sanctions for purposes with little connection to business needs. For example, at the beginning of 1997, the U.S. government enforced specific political sanctions or import penalties against 35 nations affecting nearly $4 trillion in world trade. These sanctions or penalties were imposed, aimed at coercing various countries to accept U.S. viewpoints on issues ranging from human rights to democracy, which may have deviated from the world trade perspective.

Home Government Relations with the Firm

Firms, when register as residents of particular countries, usually these home countries in which they originated, and this status causes them to be responsible for complying with the laws of those countries. Furthermore, a home country's political agenda often includes rather specific policy guidelines for foreign relations, which may inhibit the exports of certain products to protect national security. A multinational corporation cannot shun the preferences of its home country government. These firms usually must comply with the formal constraints imposed by governments on international commerce, such as boycotts, embargoes, trade sanctions, and mandates for particular terms in negotiated trade agreement. The home government have the powers can intervene in business through control measures such as import and export licensing, the regulation of foreign exchange, rulings on mergers or acquisitions, and investigations of questionable ethical behavior. International managers must comply with their home-country laws, but foreign laws take precedence for subsidiary activities.

Host Government and Home Government Relations

Political and diplomatic relations amongst countries often determine the relative risk of doing business in one country rather than another. It is clear, good relations reduce risk and encourage trade by private companies, but rapidly changing environments can often lead to variations in this risk.

In the early 1970s, for example, most Western companies considered Iran a safe haven in the turbulent Middle East. U.S-Iranian relations had long remained very stable and friendly, and many American firms had developed significant investments in Iran. This period of flourishing trade relations came to an abrupt end in 1919; however, a revolution deposed the shah of Iran and installed an extremist religious regime. The once upon a time safe haven was suddenly transformed into a nightmare of Anti-Western purging regime. These rioters took American hostages and held them in Spartan cells for more than a year, several U.S. and European businessmen were killed, and the government confiscated all foreign business assets. The reverse situation change can also take place, for instance, the collapse of soviet power and the fall of the Berlin wall abruptly ended the cold war, thus creating favorable opportunities for international investments and trade in formerly hostile markets.

Host Country External Relations

All foreign government maintains social and economic ties with other countries. However, these relationships may differ substantially from those between the host and home countries. A multinational, inexorably be monitoring and analyzing the host country's external relations. For example, a U.S. trade mission to China in 1995 discovered that U.S. electronics components exported to that country were finding their way into missile systems sold to Pakistan's strained relations between Pakistan and India led to threats of expulsion against U.S. companies with subsidiaries in India.

Government Intervention

Governments compete with each other to induce foreign investment by offering them attractive incentives to foreign firms that propel them into interventionist roles focused on steering their economies toward economic development. Their efforts to create domestic commercial environments conducive to multinational interest's amount to a direct and positive form of intervention, but as governments expand their commercial activities; they also tend to expand regulatory influence over foreign organizations. This gave rise to the love-hate scenario, that develop when governments seek control over business activities while at the same time working to entice foreign investment by multinationals. When initial relationships deteriorate, these foreign subsidiaries may suddenly find themselves in unpleasant circumstances. In some extreme cases, some firms have been expelled from the countries they originally entered at the invitation of the host government.

Intervention is not often viewed as a direct and clear activity, but rather forms on the basis of subtle regulations and controls that proliferate as a government moves toward a bureaucratic structure. Hence, most analysts would separate intervention into direct attempts to induce multinational or to exert control over them and indirect measures such as tightening export controls or influence business decisions through pressure by government agencies. Local intervention initiatives can have ramifications for a multinational corporation's networked operations in other countries.

Consequently, a multinational rarely views host-country operations in exclusive manner. More often, a firm's foreign subsidiaries represent platforms for supporting a broader range of activities.

Global Platforms and Host-Country Intervention

The comparative benefits of locating in a country or another may be important considerations an organization has to make, but international managers do not restrictively make location decisions based only on specific comparative advantages. However they evaluate how foreign subsidiaries fit into their organization's world network of activities and, in particular, how operations in specific countries can create global platforms for industry competition.

Michael Porter has explained the concept of a global platform in the following way:
A country is a desirable global platform in an industry if it provides an environment yielding firms domiciled in that country an advantage in competing globally in that particular industry......... An essential element of this definition is that it hinges on success outside the country and not merely country conditions that allow firms to successfully manage domestic competition.

The concept of a global platform has several implications. First, a particular government cannot induce foreign investment purely on the merits of its domestic markets, or their cost advantages. However it must provide the MNC a place from which to compete effectively with its global industry. Second, the MNC is likely to combine selling goods and services domestically with export sales in other markets where the host country may have competing interests. This conflict of interest can threaten relations between the host-country government and those of neighboring countries. In either situation, a host government's intervention strategies affect more than its own interests, and they sometimes conflict with the intention of competing nations with similar interests. Such competition between governments can lead to bigger disputes and charges of "beggaring thy neighbor". Third, host-country platforms established by foreign firms can undermine domestic industries and consequently host-government intervention to encourage multinational development could actually be detrimental instead of good to its economy.

For example, during the early 1980's, the French government set out to overhaul the country's entire telecommunication industry and build a competitive presence that could stand up against other European competitors. In order to attain its objective, it set up a bidding environment with extremely favorable incentives for a joint venture with a foreign MNC. The three final bidders are major telecommunications firms form Sweden, Germany, and the United States. Based on cost and technological capabilities, the obvious choice was the American firm, AT&T. However, the Germans felt that a dominant position for AT&T in France would threaten the entire European market, and they lobbied other nations to pressure France not to consider the American bid. At the same time, the French hesitated to accept AT&T's offer on political grounds. The American government, in turn, objected to Germany's intervention as well as the French government's political considerations over the business deal. After much public debates, the French selected the Swedish company's bid because it represented the least threatening choice, and the resulting alliance would not prompt political controversy with other European countries.

Risks of Direct Intervention

The analysis of political risk most often centers on the probability that foreign governments will blatantly intervene in a multinational operations. Most multinational is very concerned with loss of control over host-country activities. These may include extreme actions, such as outright confiscation of company assets, but most of the time, they are subtle interventions, such as regulatory constraints on materials procurement, government controls on licenses, and restrictions on trade permits. At the extreme end of the spectrum, intervention constitutes a direct threat to the firm's ownership, assets, property rights, and perhaps even the physical security of employees. At the subtle end of the spectrum, intervention constitutes loss of some control over operational decisions. Figure 1.2 suggests how these forms of intervention occur.

The risk of intervention increases for unstable governments in which politicians may arbitrarily change business rules and regulations. Risks are also high when an unpredictable economic environment may bring significant changes that can trigger government intervention. For example, between 1960 and 1979, 22 new governments emerged in the world as former colonial dependencies gained independence or rebels overthrow existing governments. In Iran, Cuba, Laos and Vietnam, expropriation claimed substantial foreign assets from a total of 1,535 North American and European multinationals. During the same period, the World Bank reported that 76 national governments implemented more than 500 political initiatives against MNC's resulting in substantial state ownership control over foreign assets. However, since 1979, companies have experienced relatively few incidents of expropriation or outright confiscation. New International laws and the harsh light of World War coverage have helped to deter flagrant seizure of business assets; although the threat remains, it is no longer the important risk factor that it once was.

Figure 1.2

A Spectrum of Intervention Measures

Subtle Intervention		Extreme Intervention
Licensing	Price Controls	Confiscation
Import Constraints	Content Rules	Expropriation
Export Controls	Labor Regulations	Domestication
Exchange Controls	Incentives or Penalties	Nationalization /
Specific Levies		Mandated Equity
Compliance Rules		Required Contract
General Regulation of Commerce		Foreign Taxation

Ethics and Social Responsibility

International corporations, by their very nature, are guests in foreign countries. As guests, they are expected to abide by the norms and values of their host countries. The majority of the international firms meet such requirements, and they have tried hard to become "good corporate citizens" of the countries in which they are operating. However, occasionally, the demands of the various host and home countries conflict. Consequently they often encounter "no-win situations". In other instances, the "wrong doings" of a few corporations shed doubt on the proper conduct of international corporations as a whole. Thus, the issue of the ethics and social responsibilities of international corporations, although serious, has no easy solution.

Some of the critical and controversial issues on this aspect are :-

1. Illegal payments, bribes, and corrupt practices of international corporations
2. Extraterritorial government actions and the rights of multinational corporations
3. Social, ethical, and environmental conflicts between international corporations and host and home countries.

Business Values

Business Value cannot be easily be reduced to writing. In recent years, the increase in the numbers of organizations producing statements of purpose (mission statements) has enabled observers to discuss what board of directors expect from the employees of corporations. Most statements amount to a set of aspirations, a useful means of showing those who want to know that the organization has purpose and direction. It is when such statements establishes clear codes of good practice or ethics do they really have any effect on the behavior of employees and corporations, but often in a negative way, (for example, in the resolution of disciplinary matters).

The Value of Staff

Mission statements are not the only way that employers seek to set out business values and direction. In most companies' annual reports there is a paragraph in the Chairman's statement saying how valuable the staff is to the organization. An example illustrates the point.

People are crucial to our business and we continue to invest in extensive training programmes and to establish clear objectives to enable them to achieve the Group's goals as well as their own. My thanks to all our employees for their significant contribution.
(J.M. Ic. Lixing, Chairman, John Laing Ilc; Annual Report 1995).

Board members hope that statements like this will have the effect of assuring employees that they are valued, especially when this is reflected in the pay packet and in positive annual appraisals. It is not a substitute for giving purpose to work, and it does not address the need for moral guidance when solving problems encountered in the course of day to day business.

It is in the production and implementation of code of business ethics that some of these dilemmas are being addressed in a useful and positive way. Introductions to such codes, usually signed by the Chairman or CEO, tend to be much more explicit about business values than other public document emanating from organizations. An illustration of this is in the Introduction to United Biscuits' document, "Ethics and Operating Principles":

United Biscuits' business ethics are not negotiable, a well founded reputation for scrupulous dealing is itself a priceless company asset and the most important single factor in our success is faithful adherence to our beliefs. While our tactical plans and many other elements constantly change, and basic philosophy does not. To meet the challenges of a changing world, we are prepared to change everything about ourselves except our values.

Some employees might have the mistaken concept that we do not care how results are obtained, as long as we get results. This would be wrong : we do care how we get results. We expect compliance with our standard of integrity throughout the firm, and we will support an employee who passes up an opportunity or advantage which can only be secured at the sacrifice of principle.

Where businesses have identical publicly stated values, there is a basis for expecting relationships at all levels to reflect these ideals. Most codes have sections dealing specifically with the company's relationship with its employees. These address specific areas of behavior and give guidance to resolving moral dilemmas at work.

Ethical Standard

Beside changes affecting the employee at his or her place of work, observers have noticed an important social trend in the relationship of the corporation to society. The firm is increasingly assuming a role as an upholder of ethical norms in the community.

It is apparent that general moral standards in Western countries are deteriorating. His phenomenon has been well documented and affects businesses in a number of ways. For instance, pilfering from retail stores in the States has reached epidemic proportions.

The decline in the moral climate is also reflected in the Standard of integrity of employees of all levels within the place of work. The rise in the level of complaints by supervisors and other managers about the basic honesty, discipline and respect for others of many junior employees has led to the introduction of the topic of ethical behavior into induction courses for new staff. Paradoxically, it is the failure to impart moral values by traditional agents in society, family, school, church, or other religious institutions, which is forcing the business sector to provide help in achieving minimum acceptable standards of behavior at the workplace. Professor Jack Mahoney has pointed out that Adam Smith and Montesquiess, among others, saw business as a humanizing influence in society. Mahoney himself sees no reason why this should not be encouraged. Yet, for centuries, Blake's 'dark satanic mills' and Dicken's depiction of a Victorian office in A Christmas carol has been prevailing images, with all their attendant implications for appalling conditions at the place of work (which were very often justified).

The resurgence of this role for the company, largely to fill a moral vacuum, puts special demands on senior executives. It is not surprising that some are asking "who is to act as the moral guide for the firm". This question becomes even more important in the case of multinational companies.

Social scientists point out that 'going to work' plays a significant function in the social and moral well being of employees. Studies of those who are unable to find work after being "laid off" 'reveal a pattern of social withdrawal after, say, six months; similar observations have been made of those who experience abrupt retirement. The workplace has to many, become something of a surrogate family. This dependency has implications for the firm's policy, especially in handling of change. In an age of rapid response to changing market conditions, loyalty of an employing company has become a very devalued concept.

Driven by both legislation and ethical consideration, responsible employers now provide working conditions far removed from those dark satan's mills. Simultaneously, they find themselves forced to address ethical issues concerning their staff. The workplace is increasingly seen as a place where human and social values are being cultivated, it is realized by many business leaders to be both good business sense, and good citizenship, to take account of this phenomenon. But not every business relishes this role; while some tend to be resentful of a system that forces them to do moral remedial work on the young people joining their workforce. Failure of the traditional conduits of ethical values is seen by them as a major issue which needs addressing at the highest level; they argue that most business are not well equipped to address these problem.

What are the Values of Business ?

If it is true that businesses are being forced to play an increasing role in setting or maintaining moral standards in society, then it is important to be clear about what values are inherent in them. An examination of company statements about their values shows certain recurring themes and a few 'value laden' words. Those include 'honest', 'truth', 'reputation', 'responsibility' and 'integrity'.

Few business leaders would disassociate themselves or their organizations from these concepts, though there seems to be a general reluctance to be too explicit, especially outside the United States where ethics and values play a major part in the pattern of business culture. U.S. companies seem to make a point of preparing their organization for occasions when issues of corporate moral behavior arise, the majority of U.K. corporations seem content to make broad statements about business integrity.

Comparatively few have translated their corporate values into corporate codes. The 1991 survey of the Institute of Business Ethics estimates that less them one in three of the larger United Kingdom companies have a code of business ethics, though the number is growing.

Attempts were made to discern the values which characterize corporations and their leaders. One method used was to record broad reactions to normal business challenges. Reidenbach and Robin have classified corporate attitudes in the United States in five stages, as follows:-

1. Amoral – devoid of any other value than greed
2. Legalistic – whatever is legal is O.K.
3. Responsive – enlightened self interest guides decision
4. Emerging Ethical – we wished to do what is right
5. Ethical – core values characterize all policies

An identical classification based on surveys from the 1970s, put them like this:-

1. Laissez faire – "All is fair in love, war and business"
2. Relativist – "Good ethics is good business"
3. Legalistic – "We operate according to clear rules"
4. Virtuous – "We have obligations for which we are accountable"

There is a growing interest from moral philosopher in this area. They bring with them models of human behavior which have been used to classify different attitudes and values.

There seems to be no clear agreement as to which theory best fits observed business behavior. As a result, business ethics is seen as not that relevant to real-life situations. Andrew Start, in his seminal article on business ethics in the Harvard Business Review of May 1993, observed that 'most people's motives are a confusing mix of self interest, altruism, and other influences.

Practical Ethics

What managers say they require is some practical means to resolve conflicts between economic reality and employee's wish to act as moral human beings. They contend that they are not free to be altruistic because they manage firms on behalf of others. On the other hand, they know that, in the long term, doing the right thing is good for the corporation.

The following threefold test has been offered to help resolve the ethics of a decision :-
1. Effect – who does my decision effect or hurt ?
2. Transparency – Do I mind others knowing what I have decided ?
3. Fairness – Would my decision be considered fair by those affected ?

Some business organizations are now producing tests of this sort, for example, the National Westminster Bank says :-

Key questions which may help understanding of the ethical aspects of our dealings with customers and suppliers include :-
1. Do our actions or proposed actions fall comfortably within group guidelines, the consensus view of what constitutes ethical behavior and generally accepted concepts of fairness and honesty ?
2. Might our actions mislead or raise expectations which cannot be fulfilled ?
3. Would our customer or supplier have any cause for grievances if the full extent of our actions were apparent to them ?
4. Would we have any sense of grievance if we had been treated similarly ?
5. Would an impartial observer regard our dealings as fair and honourable?

British Petroleum States that :

Within BP the general principles of individual ethical behavior include :-
1. The scrupulous avoidance of deception, 'sharp practice' fraud and of any behavior which is or might be construed to be less than honorable in the pursuit of the Group's commercial interest.
2. Honesty in dealings with BP as employer, and loyalty to BP above any and all temptations to pursue personal gain or advantage
3. Honesty and loyalty in dealing with fellow employees.
4. Respect for the trust placed in the individual including proper use of group resources of information.
5. Avoidance of the behavior or situations which may reflect badly on BP.

The value words which recur in the two firms' statements are 'fairness', 'honesty', 'respect', 'honorable', 'loyalty', and 'trust', while the word 'reputation' is implied. These words are frequently encountered in business statements and are important in establishing the prevailing ethos of the organization. This is particularly important for corporations which are transnational. Whereas a code may be useful and enforceable in a national context, the value system implied in it may be inappropriate and different elsewhere.

Cultural Relativism vs. Cultural Imperialism

One of the ways to deal with ethical concerns that arise in international business is to deny that any special considerations are requested. "When in Rome, do as the Romans do". If bribery is commonplace then it is acceptable to bribe. This doctrine, cultural relativism, is based on the reality that differences between cultures do exist. The belief is that it only makes sense to say that something is 'right' or 'wrong' in the context of a particular culture. If this were true, however, then an expatriate manager assigned to one of the pockets of the world where domestic servants are treated essentially as slaves, could herself have a slave.

Some values can only be evaluated relative to the context, but some moral norms are accepted by all. In no culture is it permissible to kill a neighbor arbitrarily (such actions could not be tolerated by any society, if only because it would surely mean that society would cease to function). There is widespread support for other basic norms, such as respecting human rights. What exactly is included as a human right is subjected to debate. Even if one argues that the areas of agreement are small, cultural relativism 'offers no persuasive' reason for seeing the international realm as a moral free-for-all in which anything goes.

At the other end of the spectrum is cultural imperialism. 'There is our way, and the wrong way'. This approach is based on justifiable stance that one must not change one's ethics to suit the business environment. Most will misinterpret this to mean that an MNC must operate in the same manner as it does at home and that MNC employees should try to assert their values on others. An expatriate manager would be correct to condemn a widespread local practice that discriminates against visible minorities. The fact that a practice is common does not make it acceptable. However, always operating with such a dogmatic approach is inappropriate, since many differences are not ethical in nature and there is no moral justification to challenge them.

For example, if a family takes their car from England to Holland, they had better be prepared to drive on the right-hand side of the road. The norms pertaining to traffic regulations are not ethical in nature, even though we may talk about driving on 'the wrong side of the road'. However, not following the local traffic laws and thereby endangering others would be unethical. This is a case where the "when in Rome" argument holds. These are business practices that, at first glance, appear to raise ethical conflicts, but under closer examination do not. A foreigner may condemn what he sees as bribery but what really may be just a different way for officials to earn part of their salary. The above two extreme views on approaching ethics in an international context have been discounted, while noting that each contains some truth.

The Need to Study International Management

The international manager will benefit much from studying what has produced successful results in the past. Though, however, researchers have reached no consensus on what factors consistently lead to successful cross-cultural management. When analyzing countries, researchers have observed some similarities and some differences in the managerial skills that have produced the best results, however they have identified no universal set of management behaviors, that is, no set of behaviors that are consistently successful no matter where applied. Within specific countries, however, some common success factors can be inferred from the behaviors that are valued in that country's corporations. Exhibit 1-1 shows the personality criteria that lead to success.

In the United States, the need to study international management is definite because the United States has been conceding its economic leadership to the Japanese in many industries – steel, automobiles, consumer electronics, and banking. Everyone speculates on why the United States is falling behind; a common topic of discussion in Washington is how to regain international competitiveness.

Research also shows that many Americans and many others that are involved in international management fail in their overseas assignments. In fact, about 16 to 40 percent return prematurely, and up to half of those who stay are considered only marginally effective by their companies. In spite of such experiences, many international firms appear complacent in their approach to management development, assuming wrongly, that what works at home will work anywhere.

Tung and Miller's study of 123 executives from large U.S firms with substantial international involvement is revealing. The study found that, although the executives acknowledge the importance of globalization and of having senior executives with international experience, international corporations are not currently committing resources to prepare executives for international assignments. This finding is consistent with some previous findings.

Japanese firms, in contrast, emphasize the use of global assignments for overall career-development purposes. At the Bank of Tokyo, one-third of the career staff gets overseas assignments specifically for this purpose, a practice also widely accepted in European firms.

Some American firms begin to realize the importance of training and experience in international management and in meeting the demands of the aggressive global competition. Duane Kullberg, CEO of Arthur Anderson, an accounting and consulting company with over half its revenue generated outside the United States, says that the company's next CEO will be 'a person with experience outside the borders of the U.S.'.

International competitiveness evolved to a level of sophistication that resulted in globalization, global competition being characterized by networks that bind these countries, institutions and people in an interdependent world-wide economy. As a result of this global economic integration, the growth rate of world trade rises faster than that of world gross domestic product.

Today's international managers are increasingly challenged by the many evolutional changes that take place in the global arena. These changes provide a complex business environment, full of opportunities but encumber with risks, in which skilled international mangers can make effective business decisions, improve interpersonal relations, and meet societal obligations. Experienced managers thrive in the international context, intuitively understanding how to gain the cooperation of foreign partners and workers.

International management is the process of planning, organizing, leading and controlling in a multicultural or cross-cultural environment. Managers increasingly recognize the importance of specialized international management skill as the workforce (both in the United States and in many other countries) becomes more diverse and as the level of investment in international business increases. International business refers to profit-related activities conducted across national boundaries. The environment for these business activities within which the International manager functions is shaped by major developments in the world.

Exhibit 1-1

Korean Chaebols' Personality Criteria for Employment

Chaebol Groups	*Employees' key success Personality traits*
Samsung	Positiveness, execution with determination, responsibility, self-motivation
Hyundai	Creativeness, thrift and diligence, future orientation.
Lucky-Goldstar	Harmonious relationships with others on the job, creativeness, foreign language, personal relationship.
Daewoo	Aggressiveness, progressiveness, sense of duty.
Ssangyong	Harmonious relationships with others on the job, personal relationship.
Korea Explosive	Harmonious relationships with others on the job, sincerity, honesty, personal relationship.
Hanjin	Creativeness, responsibility, effectiveness.
Hyosung	Sincerity, endeavor, responsibility.
Doosan	Sincerity, thrift and diligence, harmonious relationships with others on the job.
Lotte	Physical and mental soundness, adaptability, motivation to achieve.
Dongboo	Spiritedness, aggressiveness, future orientation.

Kdon

Harmonious relationships with others on the job, personal relationship, self-motivation.

Kumbo

Sincerity

Chapter Two

Strategy and Global Organizations

International Business Strategy

For many firms, even small companies, globalization of their operations play an important part in the formulation of the overall business strategy. It will be useful, therefore, at this point to introduce briefly two key components of business strategy that impact on internationalization imperatives.

Business strategy is concerned with the formulation of long-term plans by a firm to achieve its corporate mission or business objectives. These plans have many functional dimensions: economic, organizational, behavioral, production, marketing and financial. Thus business strategy is inevitably holistic in approach and seeks to integrate functional activities in order to develop appropriate policies in dealing with the changing environment at the same time preserving, and adding to, the company's advantages.

Within this framework there are two critical areas of corporate decision – making, the strategic direction of the company and the formulation of competitive strategy, that are fundamental to the achievement of corporate success. The strategic direction in essence consists of a bundle of "internalized" resources under the direction of senior management that can, at its discretion, be deployed between a number of product market or industries and geographic markets and over time, be expanded and repositioned in accordance with actual and perceived opportunities for revenue enhancement and profit gain.

The first key strategic decision for a firm is therefore to decide on what products to supply (thus determining the industries in which it operates) and the geographical spread of its operations (for example, local or regional within a particular country, nationwide within that country, international or global). The second key issue is the formulation of competitive strategy, since no matter how few or many product and geographic markets the company chooses to be in, its corporate prosperity will depend fundamentally on how well it succeeds in the individual product and geographic markets making up its business.

Strategic Direction

The product or market matrix shown in Figure 1-3 provides a framework for highlighting and analyzing the various growth opportunities open to a company. The matrix depicts products on one axis and markets on the other. Using an example let us consider a company currently specializing in the production of rayon (a celluloid fiber) in the U.S.A. which is currently sold to U.S.A. textile fabricators to be made into clothing. The matrix indicates that the company has four main strategic options (a fifth option that of vertical integration is closely linked with strategy).

Figure 1-3   Product Market Framework

		Market Present	New
Product	Present	1. – Market Penetration	2. – Market Development
	New	3.. – Product Development	4. – Diversification

1. The firm can seek to achieve a greater penetration of its existing market, increasing its share of the U.K. textile fabrication market by various competitive means (low costs and prices, product differentiation). The firm can also undertake backward integration (into supply industries) and forward integration into textile fabrication to lower costs and secure supplies and outlets. However, if the firm is already a dominant supplier, or if the market itself is mature, further growth opportunities are strictly limited.

2. The firm can aim to develop new markets for its existing products, capitalizing on the firm's production expertise. In the example, the firm can adapt rayon for use as a geo-textile (for civil engineering applications) or packaging material (cellophane firm for products such as crisps and cigarettes), or the company can globalize its operations by selling rayon in international markets.

3. The company can seek to develop new products for its existing markets, exploiting the company's marketing strengths. The company can, for example, add other synthetic fibers to its product range or blend together rayon with natural wool to create 'hybrid' fabrics of various strengths and textures for use by clothiers. This strategy however, in the case of maturity markets, suffers from the same general limitations as strategy (1).

4. The firm can aim to diversify away from its exiting activity by developing new products for new markets. The rayon firm might decide that the clothing industry had too little long-term growth potential, or that the market had become too cut-throat to make decent profit returns. In this case, disinvestment of its rayon business or a gradual move away from rayon production into say, the electronics industry may be considered. This is generally the highest risk strategy since it takes the company furthest away from its core expertise in production and expertise in marketing. All of these moves can be international in scope. As indicated in strategy (2), one obvious way for the firm to expand is by putting its existing products on foreign markets. This can be done by exporting from its U.K. production base, and employing the services to agents and distributors to handle its products in export markets. More particularly, the firm may decide to relocate production itself by establishing manufacturing plants in selected overseas markets. The company may decide to become vertically integrated on a global basis, sourcing some of its raw material requirements and intermediate products from overseas subsidiaries or suppliers, and establishing overseas sales subsidiaries in order to put its international marketing operations on a more dedicated footing. Likewise, the firm may choose to diversify its business by acquiring suitable foreign firms.

Competitive Strategy

Competitive Strategy involves the formulation of strategic plans by a firm aimed at ensuring that the firm is able to meet and beat its competitors in supplying a specific product or servicing a particular market. The main concerns of a competitive strategy are to:

1. Identify the competitive advantages and strengths of one's own firm and of rival companies.
2. Identify the characteristics and strength of the various forces driving competition in a market (Figure 1-4).

The keys to a successful competitive strategy are:

1. To understand fully what product attributes are demanded by buyers (whether it be low prices or product sophistication), with a view to
2. Establishing operationally, a position of competitive advantage, this makes the firm less vulnerable to attack either from established competitors and potential new entrants, or to erosion from the direction of buyers, suppliers and substitute products.

Competitive advantage refers to the possession by a firm of various assets and attributes (low-cost plants, innovative brands, ownership of key technologies, etc) which give it a competitive edge over rival suppliers. To succeed against competitors in winning customers on a viable (profitable) and sustainable (long-run) basis, a company must, depending on the nature of the market, be cost-effective and able to provide products offering attributes and features which customers regard as preferable to the products presented by rivals. The former enable a firm to meet and beat competitors on price, while the latter reflects the company's ability to establish product differentiation, advantages over competitors.

Internationalization can help create and sustain competitive advantages in a number of ways. For example, the cost or price advantages deriving from exporting from a centralized home production base may be negated by the imposition of tariffs or a currency appreciation. In this case, production in target markets may be more economical. Similarly, it may be advantageous to relocate production to a foreign country where labor and others input factor costs are lower than in the company's home country in order to reduce its supply costs and hence its prices. In the case of product differentiation cultural differences between countries often require companies to 'customize' their marketing effort and modify products to meet local buyer preferences. An 'in-market' presence through local manufacturing and sales subsidiaries may eventually facilitate a more effective penetration of a target market by eliminating the channel intermediaries involved in arm's length exporting. Likewise, for example, establishing a research and development (R&D) operation in an advanced industrial country may enable a company to tap into state-of-the-art developments and technologies in order to create innovative products.

Building on these competitive advantages, there are, according to Porter (1980, 1985), three main strategies for competitive success nationally and internationally: cost leadership, differentiation and focus (Figure 1-5). Low costs, particularly in commodity-type markets, help the company not only to survive a price war should one break out, but also to achieve above average profitability in more stable market conditions.

By adopting a product differentiation strategy, a company seeks to be unique within a market in a way that is valued by its customers, thus reducing the likelihood of defections to rival brands and often enabling the company to establish premium prices over competitor's offerings. General cost leadership and differentiation strategies seek to establish a competitive advantage over rival suppliers across the whole market or most of it. By contrast, focus strategies aim to build competitive advantages in narrow segments of a market, usually in terms of cost or, more usually differentiation characteristics, with niche suppliers catering for customized products or special demands.

Figure 1-4

Forces driving competition in a market

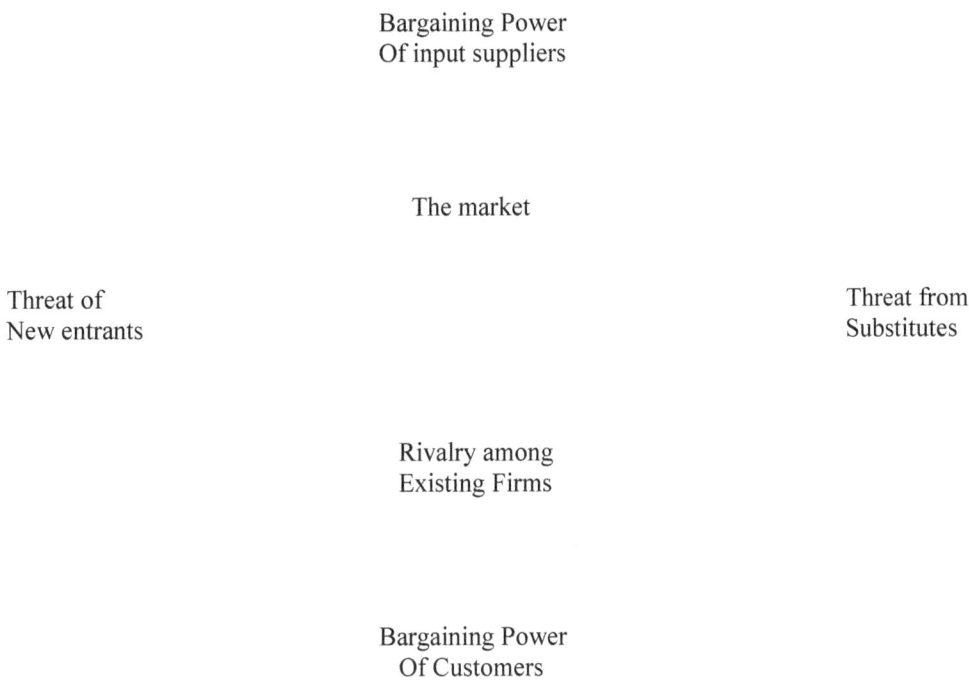

Bargaining Power
Of input suppliers

The market

Threat of   Threat from
New entrants   Substitutes

Rivalry among
Existing Firms

Bargaining Power
Of Customers

Figure 1-5

Competitive Strategy

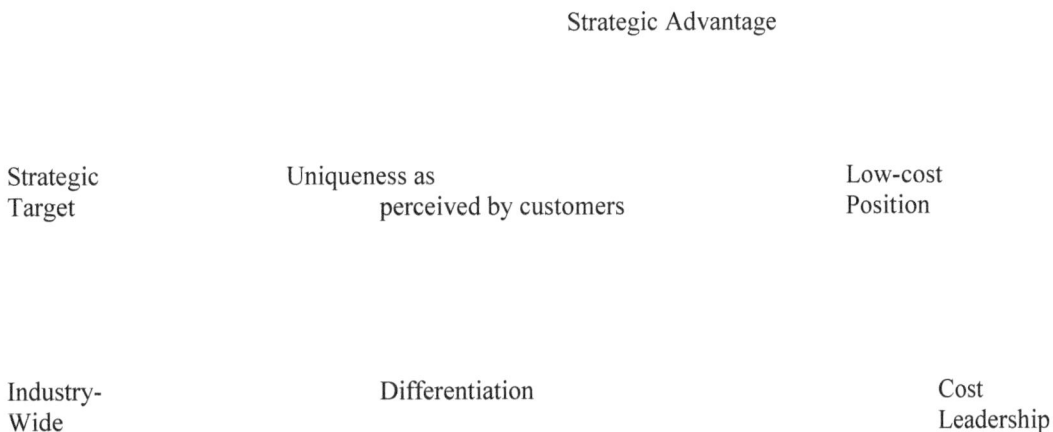

Strategic Advantage

| Strategic | Uniqueness as | Low-cost |
| Target | perceived by customers | Position |

| Industry- | Differentiation | Cost |
| Wide | | Leadership |

| Particular | Differentiation | Cost |
| Segment only | Focus | Focus |

Global Operations

Figure 1-6 illustrates a schematic summary of the foregoing discussion and how internationalization fits into the whole picture. The figure highlights two key elements of business strategy, namely, strategic direction (what business activities to engage in and the location of these activities) and competitive strategy (the means of achieving competitive success in the chosen activities). For the global scope of its activities, the firm has a number of strategic options open to it to enhance its competitiveness and sales and profit potential as illustrated in Figure 1-7.

The firm may choose to service a foreign market by exporting from a home production plant using channel intermediaries of local agents and distributors to sell its products; it may establish a company-owned sales subsidiary; or it may establish a co-marketing alliance with a foreign partner. Alternatively, the firm may decide to appoint a licensee to undertake local production or the company may decide to establish its own production subsidiary in the target market. In the case of sourcing raw materials or components (and final products), the company may decide to buy from international suppliers or it may choose to self-supply from overseas based subsidiaries as part of a networking operation.

Which of the available foreign market servicing options a company will choose, either singly or in combination, will depend on not only the general advantages and disadvantages of each particular mode, but also on an amalgam of firm-specific, industry-specific and country-specific factors, as illustrated in Figure 1-8. There is no one optimal strategy applicable to all firms or all situations. Companies differ in the resources and skills they possess, industries located in different countries vary in terms of structure and technological complexity, while countries themselves vary in terms of their industrial and market structures, stages of economic development, as well as levels of maturity.

Accordingly, it is necessary to adopt an appropriate servicing strategy in the light of individual circumstances as they exist at present and to consider altering the company's servicing mode in the light of changing firm, industry and country circumstances.

Consider the following configuration by way of example. Firm specific factors (the company has an innovative product but lacks capital); industry specific factors in the target market (the industry lacks product sophistication and has a complex distribution channel) and country-specific factors (the country is a low-wage economy and has high tariffs on imports). The only practical choice of servicing this market appears to be licensing. The firm's lack of capital rules out wholly-owned FDI (although a joint venture might be considered). High tariffs rule out solo exporting and co-marketing alliances. Licensing an established in-market player to produce the firm's product locally requires no capital outlay and gives immediate access to the distribution channels of the licensee.

Figure 1-6

Firm, industry and location factors and competitive strategy

| **Competitive Strategy** | **Firm** | **Firm-Specific factors**
(Resources, core skills and Competencies) |

Cost Leadership

| Product | Selection | Industry-Specific factors |

Differentiation   Of   (level of concentration,
                  Industry   technological complexity etc)

Focus

                  Location   Country / Location-Specific
                  Of   factors (level of wages rates,
                  Activities   size of market, etc)

Figure 1-7

Foreign market servicing and sourcing

                  Firm / Industries

                  Foreign market servicing

     Export   Strategic Alliance   Wholly-owned
                                            Foreign Direct
                                            Investment

Externalized   *** Licensee local producer**

Operation

                  * Joint Venture

                  Production Plant

Mixed   **Co-marketing**
               Alliance

                  * Co R&D alliance   **Sourcing**

       Internalized

Operation   Sales
              Subsidiary   * Components
                                             Plant

                                             * Assembly
                                             Plant

* R&D complex

Industry / Country

Figure 1-8

The Choice of foreign market servicing mode

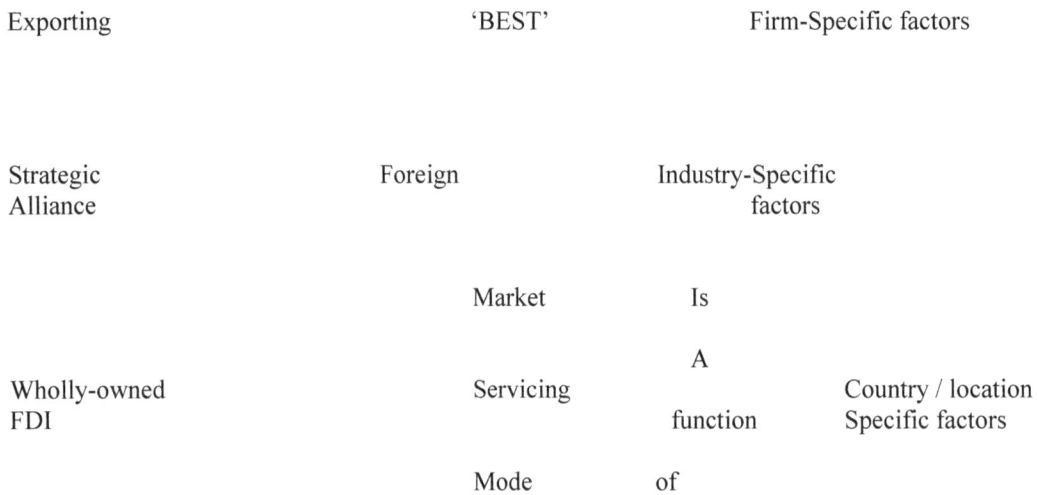

Exporting		'BEST'		Firm-Specific factors
Strategic Alliance	Foreign		Industry-Specific factors	
	Market	Is		
Wholly-owned FDI	Servicing	A function	Country / location Specific factors	
	Mode	of		

Global Organizations

As a domestic firm expands internationally, it will change its organization design to accommodate its increase international activities. To verify how this happens, we'll start by considering a domestic firm that has no international sales. This is not an unreasonable starting point. Many entrepreneurs, particularly in larger economies such as those of the United States, Japan, and Germany, start new firms in response to some perceived need in the local market; they give little immediate thought to the international market place. And many small, domestically orientated firms enter international markets passively through indirect exporting. Such a firm may sell its product to a domestic customer, and that customer then incorporates the product into a good that it distributes in foreign markets. Or, a domestic customer may purchase the final product for one of its foreign subsidiaries, or a domestic purchasing agent of a foreign wholesaler may order the firm's product. Because such indirect exporting occurs as a routine part of the firm's domestic business, the firm's organization design need not change at all.

For example, Texas-based O.I. International was started in 1969 to produce highly specialized equipment to analyze and monitor oil-drilling activities. In its early years, it had little need to think internationally because oil-drilling activity in Texas and elsewhere in the United States was booming. However, as oil field activity slowed down in the United States, O.I. needed new sources of revenue. One day, as CEO John Huey was reading a trade magazine and noticed an announcement of an industrial exhibition in Japan. He quickly made an arrangement to attend the show to promote O.I. products. During the show, he contracted with JASKO International, a Japanese equipment firm, to distribute O.I. products in Pacific Asia. There was certainly no need to overhaul the firm's structure in order to deal with this level of international involvement.

As indirect export sales grow, however, a firm may realize the value of more actively pursuing the international market. For example, one small Santa Claus, California, firm began its international sales by accident when its president unexpectedly met officials from Barno National de Mexico at a 1992 New Orleans trade fair. This chance encounter led to a $200,000 order for the firm's software for managing debt collection. Once the firm learned the tricks of doing business in Mexico, it soon expanded its marketing efforts there.

The Corollary Approach

A firm may initially respond to international sales and orders by following the corollary approach, whereby it delegates responsibility for processing such orders to individuals within an existing department, such as finance or marketing. Under this approach, the firm continues to use its existing domestic organization design. This approach is typical of a firm that has only a very small level of international activity.

Wal-Mart offers another example of the corollary approach. Wal-Mart has limited international operations and few stores outside the United States. But the firm does buy some products from foreign manufacturers. Because all of its buying is centralized in Bentonville, Arkansas, its buyers simply handle international purchases as part of their routine. Most transactions are in U.S. dollars, and shipping and transportation are the responsibility of the seller. Thus, for the Wal-mart buyer the international transaction of purchasing 10,000 VCRs from Sony for a unit cost of $200 (with freight arranged for and paid by the shipper) is fundamentally no different from buying 10,000 television from Emerson Electric (a U.S. firm) for a unit cost of $200 (with freight again arranged for and paid by the shipper). However, in responses to NAFTA, Wal-Mart entered the Mexican market in a joint venture with Mexico's largest retail chain, Citra. As its international operations increase, Wal-Mart will probably undergo restructuring in order to accommodate a larger international scope.

The Export Department

As a firm's export sales become more significant, its next step is usually to create a separate, internal export department. The export department takes responsibility for overseeing international operations, marketing products, processing orders, working with foreign distributors, and arranging financing when necessary.

Initially, the head of the export department may report to a senior marketing or finance executive. As exports grow in importance, however, the export department may achieve equality on the organization chart with finance, marketing, human resources, and the other functional areas of the firm. O.I. , for example, eventually created a small export department, comprising one manager and an assistant, to handle its exports to Japan. Figure 1-9 illustrates how an export department fits into a typical small firm.

The International Division

On a small scale, when selling to foreign customers may not be fundamentally different from selling to domestic ones, the small export department may need little or no familiarity with foreign markets. However, as international activities further increase, firms often find that an export department no longer serves their needs. Once a firm begins to station employees abroad or establish foreign subsidiaries to produce, distribute, and / or market its products, managerial responsibilities, coordination complexities and information requirements all swell beyond the export department capabilities and expertise. Familiarity with foreign markets becomes more important and new methods for organizing may be required.

Firms respond to the challenges of controlling their burgeoning international business by changing their organization design through the creation of an international division that specializes in managing foreign operations. The international division allows the firm to concentrate resources an create specialized programs and activities targeted on international business activity while simultaneously keeping that activity segregated from the firm's ongoing domestic activities. Kmart uses the international division design, in contrast to the corollary approach used by its biggest competitor, Wal-mart. Kmart has extended its retailing empire internationally, it operates stores in Canada, Puerto Rico, Mexico, and the U.S. Virgin Islands. Although its foreign outlets are outnumbered by its 2200 U.S. stores, the volume of its Canadian business in particular is quite large. To successfully manage the foreign stores, Kmart has established an international division whose managers coordinate their activities with those of managers in the firm's domestic operations. Canadian managers communicate their buying needs to regular Kmart buyers, who add the Canadian requests to their normal purchases and then route the Canadian portion to a distribution center in that country.

Figure 1-9

President and Chief Executive Officer

Director

Sales and marketing

Director

Manufacturing and Operations

Director

Export Operations

Director

Finances and Administration

Director

Human Resources and
Labor Relations

An export department in a small manufacturing firm

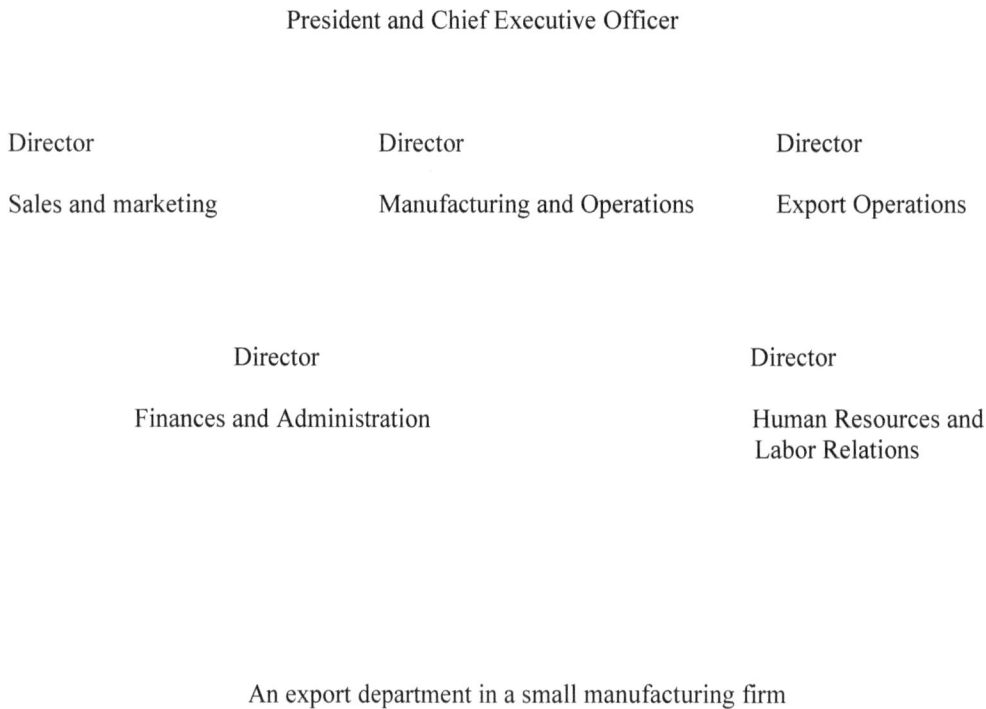

Global Strategic Planning and Organizing

Global strategic planning is the process of evaluating the firm's environment and its internal strengths, next identifying long and short range objectives, and then implementing a plan of action for attaining these goals. Multinational companies rely heavily on this process because it provides them with both general direction and specific guidance in carrying out their activities. In the absence of a strategic plan, these enterprises will have great difficulty in planning, implementing, and evaluating operations. But with strategic planning, however, research shows that many multi-corporations have been able to increase their profitability. For example, in recent years, General Motors has been very successful in both gaining market share and generating high profits in Europe. This success is due in large part to the firm's ability to formulate and implement a plan of new car introductions coupled with state-of-the-art engineering and design, improved performance quality, and careful cost control. Because of strategic planning, GM is finding Europe to be one of its most lucrative markets.

Strategic Orientations

Before studying the strategic planning process, we must recognize that MNCs have strategic predisposition toward doing things in a particular way. This predisposition helps determine the specific decisions the firm will implement.

There are four such predisposition, they are :-
1. Ethnocentric
2. Polycentric
3. Regiocenric
4. Geocentric

Table 1-3 list each predisposition and its characteristics.

An MNC with an ethnocentric predisposition will rely on the values and interest of the parent company in formulating and implementing the strategic plan. Primary emphasis will be given to profitability and the firm will try to run operations abroad the way they are run at home. This predisposition is used most commonly by firms trying to sell the same product abroad that they sell at home.

An MNC with a polycentric predisposition will tailor its strategic plan to meet the needs of a local culture. If the firm is doing business in more than one culture, the overall plan will be adapted to reflect these individual needs. The basic mission of a polycentric MNC is to be accepted by the local culture and to blend into the country. Each subsidiary will decide the objectives it will pursue, based on local needs. Profits will be put back into the country in the form of expansion and growth.

An MNC with a regiocentric predisposition will be interested in obtaining both profit and public acceptance (a combination of the ethnocentric and polycentric approaches) and will use a strategy that allows it to address both local and regional needs. The company is less focused on a particular country than on a geographic region. For example, an MNC doing business in the EC will be interested in all the member nations.

An MNC with a geocentric predisposition will view operations on a global basis. The largest international corporations often use this approach. They will produce global products with local variations and will staff their offices with the best people they can find, regardless of country of origin. Multinationals, in the true meaning of the word, have a geocentric predisposition. However, it is possible for an MNC to have a polycentric or regiocentric predisposition if the company is moderately small or limits operations to specific cultures or geographic regions.

Table 1-3

Typical strategic orientations of MNCs

MNC

Orientation	Ethnocentric	Polycentric	Regiocentric	Geocentric
Firm's basic Mission	Profitability	Public acceptance (legitimacy)	Both profitability and public acceptance	Both profitability and public acceptance
Type of Governance	Top down	Bottom up (each local unit sets objectives)	Mutually negotiated between the region and its subsidiaries	Mutually negotiated at all levels of the organizations
Strategy	Global Integration	National responsiveness	Regional integration and national responsiveness	Global integration and national responsiveness
Structure	Hierarchical product division	Hierarchical area divisions with autonomous national units	Product and regional organization tied together through a matrix structure	A network of organizations (in some cases this includes stockholder & competitors)
Culture Technology Marketing Strategy	Home country mass production Product development is determined primarily by the needs of the home country customers	Host country batch production local product development based on local needs	Regional flexible standardized within the region, but not across regions	Global flexible global products with local variations
Profit Strategy	Profits are brought back to the home country	Profits are kept in the host country	Profits are redistributed within the region	Redistribution is done on a global basis

Human Resource Management Practices	Overseas operations are managed by people from the home country	Local nationals are used in key management positions	Regional people are developed for key managerial positions anywhere in the region	The best people anywhere in the world are developed for key positions everywhere in the world

The predisposition of an MNE will greatly influence its strategic planning process. For example, some MNCs are more interested in profit and / or growth than they are in developing a comprehensive corporate strategy that exploits their strength. Some are more interested in large scale manufacturing that will allow them to compete on a price basis across the country or region, as opposed to developing a high degree of responsiveness to local demand and tailoring a product to these specific market niches. Some prefer to sell in countries where the cultures are similar to their own so that the same basic marketing orientation can be used throughout the regions. These orientations or predisposition will greatly influence the strategy.

Strategy Formulation

Strategy formulation is the process of evaluating the firm's environment and its internal strengths. This typically begins with consideration of the external arena since the MNC will first be interested in opportunities that can be exploited. Then attention will be directed to the internal environment and the resources the organization has available, or can develop, to take advantage of these opportunities.

External Environmental Assessment

The analysis of the external environment involves two activities information gathering and information assessment. These steps help to answer two key questions : What is going on in the external environment ? How will these developments affect our company?

Information Gathering

Information gathering is a critical phase of international strategic planning. Unfortunately not all firm's recognize this as an important key success factor. For example, in the case of Harley-Davidson, the large U.S. based motorcycles manufacturer, it was not until the Japanese began dominating the motorcycle market that Harley realized its problem. A systematic analysis of the competition revealed that the major reason for Japanese success in the U.S. market was the high quality of their products, a result of extremely efficient manufacturing techniques. Today Harley is competitive again. It achieved renewed success because it rethought its basic business, reformulated company strategy, vastly improved product quality, and rededicated itself to the core business : heavyweight motor cycles. Since 1983 Harley's share of the U.S. super-heavyweight motorcycle market has risen from 23 to over 50 percent.

There are a number of ways that MNCs conduct an environmental scan and then forecast the future. Four of the most common methods include :-
1. Asking experts in the industry to discuss industry trends and to make projections about the future.
2. Using historical industry trends to forecast future developments
3. Asking knowledgeable managers to write scenarios describing what they foresee for the industry over the next 2 to 3 years, and
4. Using computers to simulate the industry environment and to generate likely future developments.

Of these, expert opinion is the most commonly used. The Japanese and the South Koreans are excellent examples. Mitsubishi has over 700 employees in New York City whose primary objective is to gather information on American competitors and markets. Similar strategies are employed by all large Japanese corporations operating in the United States. The same is true for large South Korean trading firms, who require their branch mangers to send back information on market developments. These data are then analyzed and used to help formulate future strategies for the firms.

This information helps MNCs to identify competitor strengths and weaknesses and to target areas for attack. This approach is particularly important when a company is delivering a product or service for many market niches around the world that are too small to be individually profitable. In such situations the MNC has to identify a series of different niches and to attempt to market successfully in each of these geographic areas. The information is also critical to those firms that will be coming under attack.

- 51 -

Information Assessement

When information on the competition and the industry are gathered, MNCs will then assess the data. One of the most common approaches is to make an overall assessment based on the five forces that determine industry competitiveness, buyers, suppliers, potential new entrants to the industry, the availability of substitute goods and services, and rivalry among the competitors. Figure 1-10 shows the connections among these forces.

Figure 1-10

The Five Forces of Industry Competitiveness

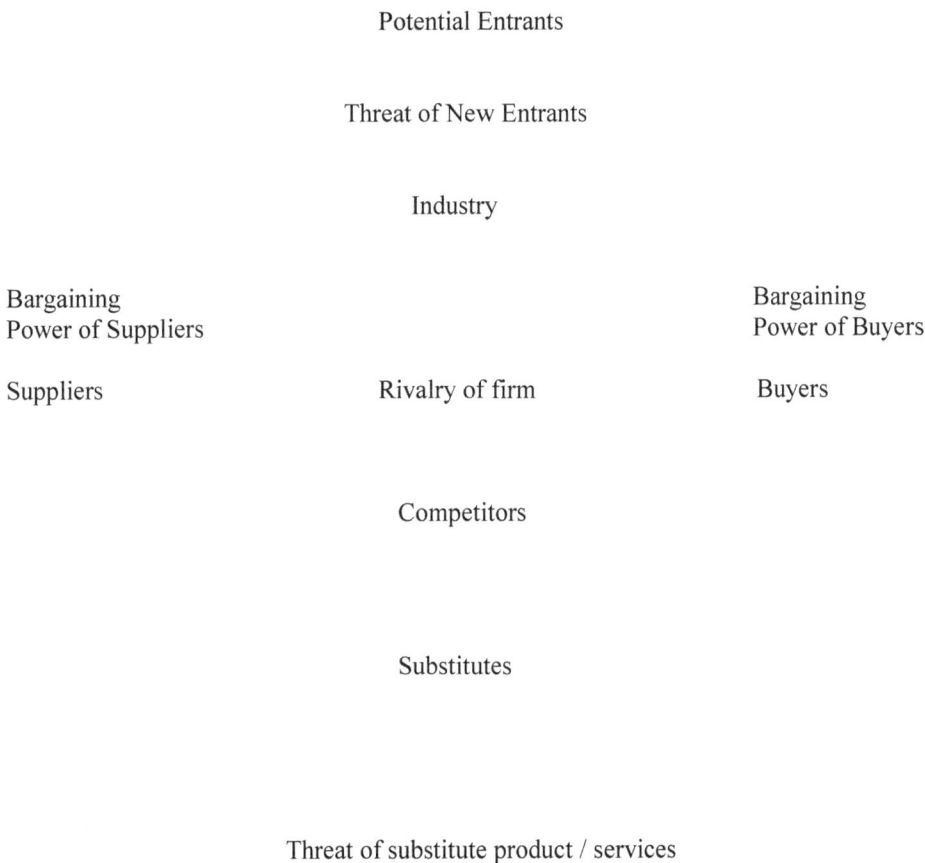

Potential Entrants

Threat of New Entrants

Industry

| Bargaining Power of Suppliers | | Bargaining Power of Buyers |

| Suppliers | Rivalry of firm | Buyers |

Competitors

Substitutes

Threat of substitute product / services

Bargaining Power of Buyers

MNCs will examine the power of their buyers because they will want to predict the likelihood of maintaining these customers. If the firm believes buyers may be moving their business to competitors, the MNC will want to formulate a strategy for countering this move. For example, the company may offer a lower price or increase the amount of service it provides.

Bargaining Power of Suppliers

An MNC will look at the power of the industry's suppliers to see if it can gain a competitive advantage here. For example, if there are a number of suppliers in the industry, the MNC may attempt to play them off against each other in an effort to get a lower price. Or the company may move to eliminate any threat from the suppliers by acquiring one of them, thus guaranteeing itself a ready source of inputs.

The New Entrants

The firm will examine the likelihood of new firms entering the industry and will try to determine the impact they might have on the MNC. Two typical ways that international MNCs attempt to reduce the threat of new entrants are by :-
1. Keeping costs low and consumer loyalty high and
2. Encouraging the government to limit foreign business activity through regulation such as duties, tariffs, quotas, and other protective measures.

The Threat of Substitutes

The MNC will look at the availability of substitute goods and services and try to anticipate when such offerings will reach the market. There are a number of steps that the firm will take to offset this competitive force, including :-
1. Lowering prices,
2. Offering similar products, and
3. Increasing services to the customer

Rivalry

The MNC will examine the rivalry that currently exists between itself and the competition and seek to anticipate future changes in this arrangement. Common strategies for maintaining and / or increasing market strength include :-
1. Offering new goods and services
2. Increasing productivity and thus reducing overall costs
3. Working to differentiate current goods and services from those of the competition
4. Increasing overall quality of goods and services and
5. Targeting specific niches with a well-designed market strategy

As the MNC examines each of these five forces, it will decide the attractiveness and unattractiveness of each. This will help the firm to decide how and where to make strategic changes.

Internal Environment Assessment

The internal environmental assessment helps to pinpoint MNC strengths and weaknesses. There are two specific areas that a multinational will examine in this assessment :-
1. Physical resources and personnel competencies and
2. The way in which value chain analysis can be used to bring these resources together in the most synergistic and profitable manner.

Physical Resources and Personnel Competencies

The physical resources are the assets that the MNC will use to carry out the strategic plan. Many of these are reported on the balance sheet as reflected by the firm's cash, inventory, machinery, and equipment accounts. However, this does not tell the entire story. The location and disposition of these resources is also important. For example, an MNC with manufacturing plants on three continents may be in a much better position to compete worldwide than a competitor whose plants are all locate in one geographic area. Location will also affect cost. In the last decade, it was possible for Japanese steel makers to sell their product in the Untied States at a lower price that could their U.S. competitors. But, since then the United States has improved its steel-producing technology and built small mini-mills that are highly efficient. Today, because of the costs of shipping the steel across the Pacific, the Japanese no longer have a cost advantage in the United States.

Another important consideration is the degree of integration that exists within the operating unit of the MNC. Large firms, in particular, are usually divided into strategic business units. In short, (SBUs). These are operating units with their own strategic space; they produce and sell goods and services to a market segment and have a well-defined set of competitors. SBUs are sometimes referred to as "business within the business." Mitsubishi, the giant Japanese conglomerate, has a host of SBUs that constitute its corporate network. These include steel making, auto production, electronics, and banking. So when a Mitsubishi SBU that manufactures and sells consumer goods is looking for help with financing, it can turn to the banking SBU. If the bank finds that a customer needs a firm to produce a particular electronics product, it can refer the buyer to the electronics SBU.

In fact, many large MNCs own assets that allow them to handle almost everything involved in producing a good or service and delivering it to the customer, known as vertical integration. Many large Japanese manufacturing firms especially have moved toward vertical integration by purchasing controlling interests in their suppliers. The objective is to obtain control over the supply and to ensure that the materials or goods are delivered as needed. Many U.S. and European firms have refrain from this strategy because "captured suppliers" are usually less cost effective than independents. For example, a decade ago, Time magazine owned the forests for producing the paper it needed. However, the firm eventually sold this resource because it found that the cost of making the paper was higher than that charged by large paper manufacturers that specialize in this product. Hence, vertical integration may reduce costs in some instances, but it can be an ineffective strategy in other cases. One outstanding set back, which vertical integration is defending itself is that there are cases where the competitors in the same industry who are less vertically integrated were able to achieve cost efficiencies than those who were.

Personal competencies are the abilities and talents of the people. An MNC will want to examine these because they reflect the firm's strength and weaknesses. For example, if the firm has an innovative R&D department, it may be able to develop high quality, state-of-the-art products. However, if the firm has no sales department, it will sell the output to a firm that can handle the marketing and distribution. Generally, if a company lacks a strong R&D department but has an international sales force, it may allow the competition to bring out new products and to rely on its own R&D people to reverse engineer them, that is to find out how they are built and to develop technologies that can compete and excel. This strategy has been used by many internationally based personal computer (PC) firms that have taken PC technology and used it to develop similar, but far less expensive, units that are now beginning to dominate the world market. Not every NNC has the personnel competencies to be first in the field, and many are satisfied to follow because the investment risk is less and the opportunity for profit is usually good.

Value Chain Analysis

A complementary approach to internal environment assessment is an examination of the firm's value chain. A value chain is the way in which primary and support activities are combined in providing goods and services and in increasing profit margins. Figure 1-11 illustrates the general scheme of a value chain. The primary activities in this chain include:-
1. Inbound logistics such as receiving, storing, materials handling, and warehouse activities.
2. Operations in which inputs are put into final product form by performing activities such as machining, assembling, testing, and packaging
3. Outbound logistics which involves distributing the finished product to the customer;
4. Marketing and sales which are used to encourage buyers to purchase the product, and
5. Service for maintaining and enhancing the value of the product after the sale through activities such as repair, product adjustment, training, and parts supply.

The support activities in the value chain consist of :-
1. The firm's infrastructure, which is made up of the company's general management, planning, finance, accounting, legal, government affairs, and quality management areas;

2. Human resource management, which is made up of the selection, placement, appraisal, promotion, training, and development of the firm's personnel;
3. Technology in the form of knowledge, research and development, and procedures that can result in improved goods and services; and
4. Procurement, which involves the purchasing of raw materials, suppliers and similar goods.

MNCs can use these primary and support activities to increase the value of the goods and services they provide. In this way, they form a value chain. An example is illustrated in Figure 1-12, which helps to explain why IBM has been so effective in the international market. The firm combines the primary and support activities so as to increase the value of its products. IBM's alliance with ROLM and MCI and its strengths in software and hardware technologies provide the firm with a solid foundation for launching successful strategies in the telecommunications industry.

This idea of a value chain can be applied by any firm. For example, Makita of Japan has become a leading competitor in power tools because it was the first to use new, less expensive materials for making tool parts and to product in a single plant standardized models that it then sold worldwide.

Figure 1-11

A Basic Value Chain

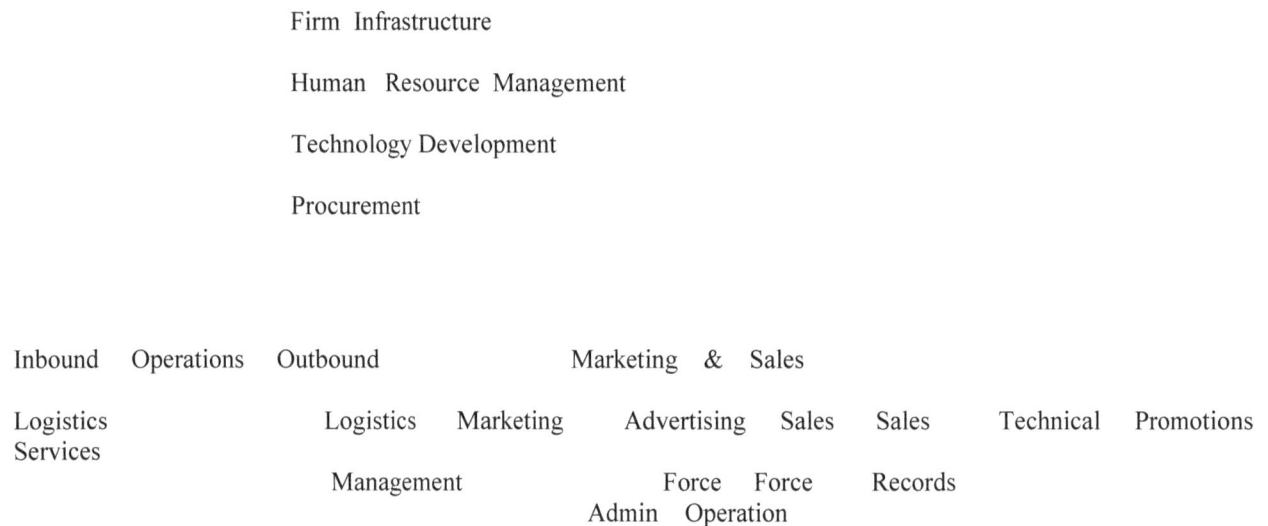

Firm Infrastructure

Human Resource Management

Technology Development

Procurement

Inbound	Operations	Outbound		Marketing & Sales					
Logistics Services		Logistics	Marketing	Advertising	Sales	Sales	Technical	Promotions
		Management			Force Admin	Force Operation	Records	

Figure 1-12

The Value Chain for IBM

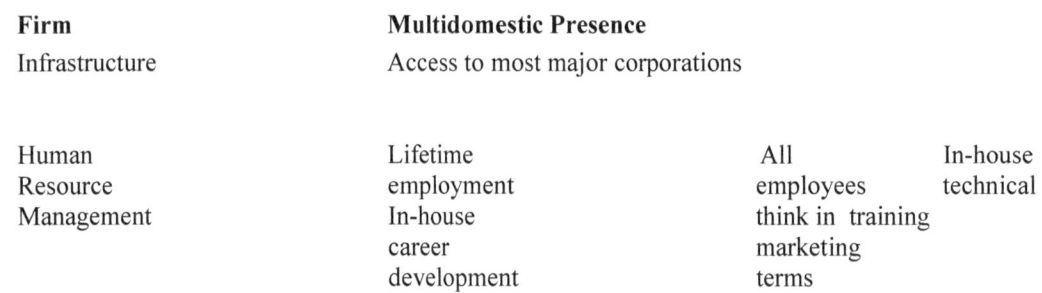

Firm Infrastructure	**Multidomestic Presence** Access to most major corporations		
Human Resource Management	Lifetime employment In-house career development	All employees think in marketing terms	In-house technical training

- 54 -

Technology Development		Strong R&D resources	Strong software capability		
Procurement	Owns ROLM (CPE manufacturer)				
		Leading computer technology used in-house partnership with MCI	Strong reputation for excellence already sells to most major corporations experienced sales force	Extensive buyer training	
	Inbound Logistics	Operations	Outbound Logistics	Marketing & Sales	Service

Analysis of the value chain can help a firm to determine the type of strategy that will be most effective. In all, encapsulated are three generic strategies :-
1. Cost
2. Differentiation, and
3. Focus

Cost Strategy

Relies on such approaches as aggressive construction of efficient facilities, vigorous pursuit of cost reductions and overhead control, avoidance of marginal customer accounts, and cost minimization in areas like R&D, Service, Sales, and advertising.

Differentiation Strategy

Is directed toward creating something that is perceived as being unique. Approaches to differentiation can take many forms, including the creation of design or brand image, improved technology or features, and increased customer service or dealer networks.

Focus Strategy

This involves concentrating on a particular buyer group and segmenting that niche based on product line or geographic market. While low cost and differentiation strategies are aimed at achieving objectives industry wide, a focus strategy is built around servicing a particular target market, and each functional policy is developed with this in mind.

In addition, the firm will determine its competition scope, which is the breadth of its target within the industry. The value chain can help an MNC to create synergies within the organization's activities. For example, by combining the human resource talent of its European salespeople with the design expertise of the design and styling people, Ford Motor has been able to design cars for the EC countries that are as competitive as those built by local firms. Similarly, IBM relies heavily on its Swiss R&D facilities to produce technological breakthrough that can be used in the machines it sells worldwide. By analyzing the ways of combining primary and support activities, MNCs will build a strategy that allows them to use their strengths and to minimize their weaknesses.

Objective Setting

The external and internal environmental analyses will provide the MNC with the information needed for setting goals. Some of these goals will be determined during the external analysis, as the company identifies opportunities that it wants to exploit. Others will be finalized after the value chain analysis is complete. In either event one of the outcomes of strategy formulation will be the identification of goals.

There are two basic ways of examining the goals or objectives of international business operations. One is to review them on the basis of operating performance or functional area. Table 1-4 provides an illustration. Some of the major goals will be related to profitability, marketing, production, finance, and human resources. A second way is to examine these goals by geographic area or on an SBU basis. For example, the European group may have a profitability goal of 16 percent, the North American group's profitability goal may be 17 percent, and the Pacific Rim group's goal may be 18 percent. Then there will be accompanying functional goals for marketing, production and finance. If the MNC has SBUs, each strategic business unit in these geographic locales will have its own list of goals.

This approach uses what is called a "cascading effect" because, like a cascade of water rippling down the side of a hill, it reaches the bottom by moving from one level to the next. The MNC will start out by setting a profitability goal for the overall enterprise. Each geographic area or business unit will then be assigned a profitability goal which, if attained, will result in the MNC reaching its overall desired profitability.

The same approach will be used in other key areas such as marketing, production, and finance. Within each unit, these objectives will then be further sub divided so that every part of the organization understands its objectives and everyone is working toward the same overall goals.

Table 1-4

Typical Goals of an MNC

Profitability	Marketing	Production	Finance
Level of products	Total sales volume	Ratio of foreign to	Financing of foreign
Return on assets,	Market share	domestic production	affiliates-retained
investment, equity,	Worldwide, region	share	earnings or local
sales	country	Economies of Scale	borrowing
Annual profit	Growth in Sales	via international	Taxation-minimizing
growth	Volume	production integration	the burden globally
Annual earnings	Integration of	Quality and cost	Optimum capital
per share, growth	country markets	Control	Structure
	for marketing	Introduction of	Foreign exchange
	efficiency and	Cost-efficiency	management-
	effectiveness	production methods	minimizing losses
			from foreign
			fluctuations

Human resource
Management
Development of
Managers with
Global orientation
Management
development of host country nationals

Going Global and Applying Strategies

Strategy Implementation

Strategy implementation is the process of obtaining goals by using the organizational structure to execute the formulated strategy properly. There are many areas of focus in this process. Three of the most important are location, ownership decisions, and functional area implementation.

Location

Over the past decade MNCs have expanded their international presence. Some of the areas in which they have begun to set up operations include China, the former Soviet Union, and Eastern Europe.

Location is important for various reasons. Local facilities often provide a cost advantage to the producer. This is usually true when the raw materials, parts, or labor needed to produce the product can be inexpensively obtained close to the facility. Location is also important because residents may prefer locally produced products. For example, many people in the United States like to "buy American". Some locations may be attractive because the local government is encouraging U.S. investment through various means such as low tax rates, free land, subsidized energy and transportation rates, and low-interest loans. Imported goods may be subject to a tariff, quota, or other governmental restriction, making local manufacture more desirable. Finally, the MNC may already be doing so much business in a country that the local government will insist that it set up local operations and begin producing more of its goods internally. This is one of the major reasons that Japanese auto manufacturers have started to establish operations in the United States.

Although the benefits are great, there are also a number of drawbacks associated with placing operations overseas. An unstable political climate may leave an MNC vulnerable to low profits and bureaucratic red tape. In Russia, for example, the government has encouraged joint ventures, but because of political and economic uncertainty, many business people currently regard Russian investments as highly risky ventures. A second drawback is the possibility of revolution or armed conflict. In Liberia, for example, the government was recently overthrown and many MNCs found their business operations suffering as a result of lost sales. MNCs with operations in Kuwait lost just about all of their investment in the Gulf War, and MNCs with locales in Saudi Arabia and other mid-east countries affected by the Gulf War also withstood losses in the region.

Ownership

Ownership of international operations has become an important issue in recent years. Many Americans, for example, believe that the increase in foreign-owned business in the United States is weakening the economy. People in other countries have similar feelings about U.S. business there. In truth, the real issue of ownership is whether or not the company is contributing to the overall economic good of the country where it is doing business. As one researcher noted recently "....because the U.S. owned corporation is coming to have no special relationship with Americans, it makes no sense for the United States to entrust our national competitiveness to it. The interests of American-owned corporations may or may not coincide with those of the American people. Countries that want to remain economically strong must be able to attract international investors who will provide jobs that allow their workers to increase their skills and build products that are demanded on the world market. In achieving this objective, two approaches are now in vogue : international joint ventures and strategic alliances.

International Joint Ventures

An international joint venture is an agreement between two or more partners to own and control an overseas business. There are a number of reasons for the rise in popularity of these ventures. One is government encouragement and legislation, designed to make it attractive for foreign investors to bring in local partners. A second is the need for partners who know the local economy, the culture, and the political system and who can cut through red tape in getting things done. A third is a desire to find partners who have local operations that can create a beneficial synergy with an outside company. For example, an MNC might provide a local partner with technology know-how and an infusion of capital that will allow the local firm to expand operations, increase market share, and begin exporting. The synergy created by the two firms can be profitable to each.

Unfortunately, in many cases, international joint ventures have not worked out well. Several studies indicate a failure rate of 30 percent for ventures in developed countries and 45 to 50 percent in less developed countries. The major reason has been the desire by MNCs to control the operation ,which sometimes has resulted in poor decision making and / or conflicts with the local partners. In general, joint ventures are difficult to manage and are frequently unstable. This is probably why many MNCs have turned to the use of strategic partnerships.

Strategic Partnerships

A strategic partnership is an agreement between two or more competitive MNCs for the purpose of serving a global market. In contrast to a joint venture where the partners may be from different businesses, strategic partnerships are almost always formed by firms in the same line of business. A good example is the General Motors and Toyota partnership that builds small cars in the United States. Other strategic agreements in the industry have brought together Nissan and Subaru, Volkswagen and Audi, Chrysler and Mitsubishi, and Ford Motor and Mazda. Strategic partnerships are also gaining popularity in other industries. For example, Motorola and Toshiba have a manufacturing facility in Japan, and they exchange a broad range of microprocessor and memory chip technology. Motorola is strong in the microprocessor area and Toshiba is a leader in chip technology, so the strategic alliance has benefits for both firms.

These alliances help to illustrate the growing popularity of international business ownership agreements. The final determinant will always be whether the arrangement is in the best interests of all involve parties. When it is, then a strategic alliance is likely to be formed.

Functional Strategies

Functional strategies are used to coordinate operations and to ensure that the plan is carried out properly. Whilst the specific functions that are key to the success of the MNC will vary, they typically fall into six major areas:-
1. Marketing
2. Manufacturing
3. Finance
4. Procurement
5. Technology
6. And Human Resources

For purposes of analysis, they can be examined in terms of three major considerations : Marketing, Manufacturing and Finance.

Marketing

The marketing strategy is designed to identify consumer needs and to formulate a plan of action for selling the desired goods and services to these customers. Most marketing strategies are built around what is commonly known as the "four P's" of marketing : product, price, promotion, and place. The company will identify the products that are in demand in the market niches they are pursuing. It will apprise the manufacturing department of any modifications that will be necessary to meet local needs, and it will determine the price at which the goods can be sold. Then the company's attention will be devoted to promoting the products and to selling them in the local market.

Manufacturing

The manufacturing strategy is designed to dovetail with the marketing plan and to ensure that the right products are built and delivered in time for sale. Manufacturing will also coordinate its strategy with the procurement and technology people, so as to ensure that the desired materials are available and that the products have the necessary state-of-the-art quality. If the MNC is producing goods in more than one country, it will be giving attention to coordinating activities where needed. For example, some firms produce goods in two or more countries and then assemble and sell them in other geographic regions. Japanese auto firms send car parts to the United States for assembly and then sell some of the assembled cars in Japan. Whirlpool builds appliances worldwide with operations in Brazil, Canada, Mexico, the Netherlands, and seven other countries. Such production and assembly operations have to be coordinated carefully.

Finance

Financial strategies used to be formulated and controlled out of the home office. However, in recent years MNCs have learned that this approach can be cumbersome, and, because of fluctuating currency prices, it can be costly. Today overseas units have more control over their finances than before, but they are guided by a carefully constructed budget that is in accord with the overall strategic plan. They are also held to account for financial performance in the form of return on investment, profit, capital budgeting, debt financing, and working capital management. The financial strategy often serves both to lead and lag the other functional strategies. In the lead position, finance limits the amounts of money that can be spent on marketing (new product development, advertising, promotion) and manufacturing (machinery, equipment, quality control) to ensure that the desired return on investment is achieved. In the lag position the financial strategy is used to evaluate performance and to provide insights regarding how future strategy should be changed.

Control and Evaluation

The strategy formulation and implementation process are a prelude to control and evaluation. The control and evaluation process involves an examination of the MNC's performance for the purpose of determining
1. How well the organization has done and
2. What actions should be taken in light of this performance. This process is tied directly to the overall strategy in that the objectives serve as the basis for comparison and evaluation. Figure 1-13 illustrates how this process works.

If the comparison and evaluation show that the strategic business unit or overseas operation is performing according to expectations, then things will continue as before. The objectives may be altered because of changes in the strategic plan, but otherwise nothing major is likely to be done. On the other hand, if there have been problems, the MNC will want to identify the causes and work to eliminate or minimize them. Similarly, if the unit has performed extremely well and achieved more then forecasted, the management may want to reset the objectives to a higher level because there is obviously greater market demand then was believed initially. In making these decisions, the company will use a variety of measures. Some will be highly quantitative and depend on financial and productivity performance; others will be more qualitative and judgemental in nature. There are six most commonly used methods of measurement for control and evaluation purposes.

Common Methods Of Measurement

Specific methods of measurement will vary depending on the nature of the MNC and the goals it has established. However, in most cases return on investment (ROI), which is measured by dividing net income before taxes by total assets, is a major consideration. There are a number of reasons that ROI is so popular as a control and evaluation measure. These include the fact that ROI :
1. Is a single comprehensive result that is influenced by everything that happens in the business.
2. Is a measure of how well the managers in every part of the world are using the investments at their command, and
3. Allows a comparison of results among units in the same country as well as on an inter-country basis. Of course, there are shortcomings in using ROI, such as that
    A) if one unit is selling goods to another unit, the ROI of the former is being artificially inflated;
    B) the ROI in a growing market will be higher than that in markets which are just getting off the ground or which are maturing, so that a comparison of the ROI performance between units can be misleading, and
    C) the ROI is a short-term measure of performance, and if it is relied on too heavily, managers will not develop the necessary long-term time horizons. Although it encumbrances such shortcomings, however, the ROI remains a major measure of performance.

Another measure is sales growth and / or market share. Units will be given sales targets that usually require greater sales this year then last year. If the firm has made an estimate of the total demand, a market share figure will accompany the sales target. The reason for this is twofold:
1. the MNC wants to increase its sales and
2. the firm wants at least to maintain, if not increase, market share. If the market is judged to be declining, sales target will be lowered but the MNC will still try to maintain market share.

A third performance area is costs. The MNC will want to achieve increased sales and market share at as low a cost as possible. The firm will also want to maintain close control of production costs. So expenses will be monitored carefully. This is particularly important in declining markets, where the company will want to cut costs as sales decline. For example, if an MNC estimates that it has but 3 years of product life in the market, it is likely that much of the advertising and promotion expenses will be dropped as the company focuses attention on supplying an ever decreasing number of customers. This strategy is often successful because the remaining customers are highly loyal and do not need promotional efforts to convince them to buy the product.

New product development is another area of performance measure. This area is extremely important for firms that rely on new offerings. A good example is Nintendo, the Japanese manufacturer of such well-known video games as Mario Brothers. In order to maintain market share and sales growth, the company must continually introduce new product offerings. MNEs in high-tech areas such as electronic goods and computers also fall into this category. In an environment where product improvement or innovation is critical to success, new product development is a key area for control and evaluation.

MNC/host country relations is another performance area that must be evaluated. Overseas units have to work within the cultural and legal framework of the host country. Many attempt to do this by blending into the community, hiring local managers and employees, adapting their product to the demands of that market, reinvesting part (if not all) of their profits back into the country, and working to improve the economic conditions of the area. As a result, they get on well in the country and there are no problems with the government or other local groups. One thing MNCs know from long experience is that poor host country relations can seriously endanger profits and many result in a loss of invested capital.

Finally, management performance must be considered. In rating this criterion, the MNC will consider two types of measures:-
1. Quantitative and
2. Qualitative

In the quantitative area, in addition to those discussed above, other common considerations included return on invested capital and cash flow. In the qualitative area, in addition to host country relations, considerations will be given to relations with the home office, the leadership qualities of the unit's managers, how-well the unit is building a management team, and how well the managers of the unit have implemented the assigned strategy. These methods of measurement will be used in arriving at an overall assessment of the unit's performance. Based on the results, the MNE will then set new goals and the international strategic planning process and agenda.

Figure 1-13

THE CONTROL AND EVALUATION PROCESS.

Identification
Of goals and other
End points to be
Measured

Establishment
of predetermined
standards

Measurement
of these
standards

Continue
As before

Does the
performance
match the
standards

Take

Corrective action

Designing Effective and Responsive International Firms

As a firm evolves from domestically oriented with international operations to becoming a true multinational corporation with global aspirations, it typically abandons the international division approach. In place of that division, it usually creates a global organization design to achieve synergies among its far flung operations and to implement its organizational strategy. The five most common forms of global organization design are product, area, functional, customer, and matrix. The global design, the MNC choices will reflect its need for coordination among its units, the source of its firm-specific advantages, and is managerial philosophy about its position in the world economy. MNCs usually adopt one of three managerial philosophies that guide their approach to such functions as organization design and marketing.

The ethnocentric approach is used by firms that operate internationally the same way they do domestically. The polycentric approach is used by firms that customize their operations for each foreign market they serve. Finally, the geocentric approach is used by firms that analyze the needs of their customers worldwide and then adopt standardized operations for all markets they serve. Figure 1-14, illustrates a typical bank, International Division Design.

Global Product Design

The most common form of organization design adopted by MNCs is the global product design. The global product design assigns worldwide responsibility for specific products or product groups to separate operating divisions within a firm. This design works best when the firm has diverse product lines or when its product lines are sold in diverse markets, thereby rendering the need for coordination between product lines relatively unimportant. If the products are related, the organization of the firm takes on what is often called an M-form design; if the products are unrelated, the design is called an H-form design. The M in M-form stands for 'multinational" – the various divisions of the firm are usually self-contained operations with interrelated activities. The H in H-form stands for "holding", as in "holding company" – the various unrelated businesses function with autonomy and little interdependence. The global product design adopted by Daimler-Benz is illustrated in Figure 1-15. This firm's various businesses are relatively unrelated, thus it uses the H-form design.

Another MNC that uses the global product approach is Philip Morris. This firm makes a wide variety of products, ranging form Marlboro cigarettes to Cool Whip to Jell-O to Oscar Mayer Bologna to Toblerone chocolate to Miller Beer. As a result, Philip Morris uses the global product design, organizing its operations along product lines. Its major divisions include tobacco, brewing, and food processing. Although most of its manufacturing and processing are done in the United States, in order to achieve economies of scale, separate groups of product oriented managers are then responsible for marketing a single product or related group of product to all markets the firm serves. Because each group is some-what related to the others, Philip Morris exemplifies the M-form design.

Pennsylvania's Harsco Corporation, too, is organized according to its major product groups – industrial services and building products, engineering products, and defense products. Each group is responsible for managing domestic and international production, marketing, and distribution for its individual product lines. The global product design has several advantages :-
1. Because a division focuses on a single product or product group, the division managers gain expertise in all aspects of the product or products.
2. It facilitates efficiencies in production because managers are free to manufacture the product wherever manufacturing costs are the lowest.
3. It allows managers to coordinate production at their various facilities, shifting output from factory to factory as global demand or cost conditions fluctuate.
4. Because managers have extensive product knowledge, they are more able to incorporate new technologies into their product (s) and respond quickly and flexibly to technological changes that affect their market.

Not surprisingly, as competition in their industry intensified in the 1990s, two major personal computer manufacturers – IBM and Siemens Nixdorf – switch to the global product design. These firms operate in an industry environment characterized by vicious price competition, global sourcing of inputs, and rapid technological change. Within months of IBM's restructuring, the firm noticed a significant difference in its ability to respond to its competitors. For example, when Compaq launched a price war in summer 1992, IBM was able to counterattack within two hours with its own price units, a decision that would have taken several weeks under its old structure.

The global product design offers other advantages :-
1. It facilitates global marketing. The firm gains flexibility in how it introduces, promotes, and distributes each product or product group. Rather than being tied to one marketing plan that encompasses the whole firm, individual product-line managers may pursue their own plans.

2. It enables the firm to develop specific expertise needed to compete globally. In Harsco's case, one of the firm's competitive advantages lies in its specialized knowledge of how to convert steel mill waste into useful products. Using the global product design, Harsco can focus this experience within its industrial services and building products group, which can then use this knowledge to compete internationally for contracts with steel mills.
3. Because the global product design forces managers to think globally, it facilitates geocentric corporate philosophies. This is a useful mind-set as firms work to develop greater international skills internally.

The global product design also has its limitations
1. It may encourage expensive duplication, since each product group needs its own functional area skills such as marketing, finance, and information management and sometimes even its own physical facilities for production, distribution, and R&D.
2. Each product group must develop its own knowledge about the cultural, legal, and political environments of the various regional and national markets in which it operates.
3. It makes coordination and corporate, learning across product groups more difficult. If such coordination is an important part of the firm's international strategy, it may want to adopt a different global design, such as global area design.

Figure 1-14

International Division Design

President and Chief Executive Officer

Vice President	Vice President	Vice President	Vice President
Corporate finance	Retail Banking	Corporate Banking	International
And Non-financing	Division	Division	Banking
Investment			Division

Figure 1-15

Daimler-Benz's Global Product Design

Daimler Benz

Corporate   Staff

Administration   **Functions**

Debris (Daimler-Benz interservice)	Mercedes Benz	Aeg	Deutsche Aerospace
Computing And Communication Services	Passenger Cars	Automation	Aircraft
Financial Services	Commercial Vehicles	Rail Systems	Space Systems
Insurance		Domestic Appliances	Defense Systems

Trading	Electro-technical	Propulsion Systems Systems and Components
Marketing Services	Micro-Electronics	Other Activities
		Office and Communication Systems

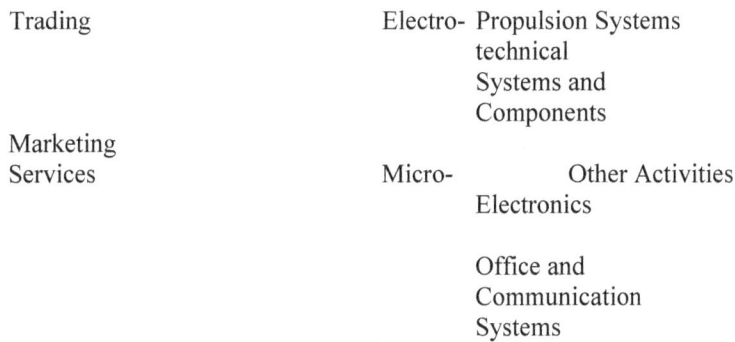

Global Area Design

The second most common form of global design is the global area design. The global area design organizes the firm's activities around specific areas or regions of the world. This approach is particularly useful for firms with a polycentric or multi-domestic corporate philosophy. Figure 1-16 illustrates a part of "Nestle" that is organized by area. Note that the president and chief operating officer of the firm's food division oversee five directors, each of whom is responsible for a specific geographical area. Thus, while the top level of the firm is organized by product, the food division itself is organized by area.

A global area design is most likely to be used by a firm whose products are not readily transferable across regions. For example, Bertelsmann AG is the world's largest media firm; it publishes newspapers and magazines and records music and video materials. Because of language differences and cultural preferences, however, a Bertelsmann magazine published in the United States cannot be exported in large quantities for sale in Germany or Japan. Thus the firm has separate headquarters in each country in which it operates. The U.S. headquarters, for example, oversees publication of books under the mastheads of Bantam, Dell, and Doubleday and of magazines such as Parents and Young Miss and records music under such labels as Aristae and RCA. Similarly, Bertelsmann's German operation publishes books under the label Bertelsmann club, publishes magazines such as Deer Spiegel, and records music by the Label BMG Areola.

The global area design does have limitations, however:
1. By focusing on the needs of the area market, the firm may sacrifice cost efficiencies that might be gained through global production.
2. Diffusion of technology is slowed, for innovations generated in one area division may not be adopted by all the others. Thus this design may not be suitable for product lines undergoing rapid technological change.
3. The global area design results in duplication of resources because each area division must have its own functional specialists, product experts, and, in many cases, production facilities.
4. It makes coordination across areas expensive and discourages global product planning.

Figure 1-16

GLOBAL AREA DESIGN OF NESTLE'S FOOD DIVISION

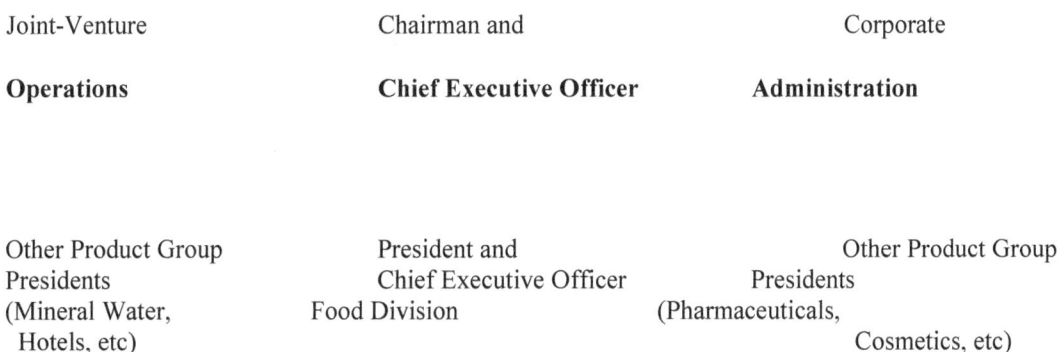

Joint-Venture **Operations**	Chairman and **Chief Executive Officer**	Corporate **Administration**
Other Product Group Presidents (Mineral Water, Hotels, etc)	President and Chief Executive Officer Food Division	Other Product Group Presidents (Pharmaceuticals, Cosmetics, etc)

Director Director Director Director Director

Zone 1	Zone 2	Zone 3	Zone 4	Zone 5
(Europe)	(Asia & Oceania)	(Latin America)	(North America)	(Africa & Middle East)

In fact, these were the reasons that led Ford to abandon its global area design in favor of a global functional design.

Global Functional Design

The global functional design calls for a firm to create departments or divisions that have worldwide responsibility for the common organizational functions, like finance, operations, marketing, R&D, and human resources management. This design is used by MNCs that have relatively narrow or similar product lines. It results in what is often called a U-form organization, where the U stands for "unity". An example of the global functional design is that used by British Airways, as shown in Figure 1-17. This firm is essentially a single-business firm, it provides air transport services, and has company-wide functional operations dedicated to marketing and operations, pubic affairs, engineering, corporate finance, human resources, and other basic functions.

The global functional design offers several advantages :-
1. The firm can easily transfer expertise within each functional area. For example, production skills learned by Exxon's crews operating in the Gulf of Mexico can be used by its offshore operations in Malaysia's Jerneh field, and new catalytic cracking technology tested at its Baton Rouge, Louisiana, refinery can be adopted by its refineries in Singapore and Trecate, Italy.
2. Managers can maintain highly centralized control over functional operations. For example, the head of Exxon's refinery division can rapidly adjust the production runs or product mix of refineries to meet changes in worldwide demand, thereby achieving efficient usage of these very expensive corporate resources.
3. The global functional design focuses attention on the key functions of the firm. For example, managers can easily isolate a problem in marketing and distinguish it from activities in other functional areas.

These advantages led Ford to adopt the global functional design. Despite these advantages, however, this design is inappropriate for many businesses. In particular, this organization design has three major shortcomings.

It is practical only when the firm has relatively few products or customers. Coordination between divisions can be a major problem. For example, the manufacturing division and the marketing division may become so differentiated from each other that each may start pursuing its own goals to the detriment of the firm as a whole.

There may be duplication of resources among managers. For example, the finance, marketing, and operations managers may each hire an expert on Japanese regulation, when a single expert could have served all three functional areas just as effectively.

Because of these problems, the global functional design has limited applicability. It is used by many firms engaged in extracting and processing natural resources, such as in the mining and energy industries, because in their case the ability to transfer expertise is important. Firms that need to impose uniform standards on all of their operations may also adopt this approach. For example, to assure safety, British Airways standardizes its maintenance and flight procedures regardless of whether a flight originates in London, Hong Kong or Sydney.

Figure 1-17

British Airways's Global Functional Design

Chairman and

Chief Executive Officer

Director Marketing & Operations	Director Public Affairs	Director Engineering	Director Health Services	Director Government & Industry Affairs	Director Safety, Security and Environment
Director Flight Crew Operations	Director Corporate Strategy	Director Corporate Finance	Director Legal Affairs	Director Human Resources	

Global Customer Design

The global customer design is used when a firm serves different customers or customer groups, each with specific needs calling for special expertise or attention. For example, the marketing operation of NEC, Japan's largest manufacturer and supplier of telecommunications equipment, uses the global customer design (see Figure 1-18). As a figure shows, Nippon Telephone and Telegraph, Japan's public telephone service and NEC's largest customer, is so important to the firm that it has a separate sales director and department dedicated exclusively to servicing the account. The firm also has separate marketing groups for government and public sector sales, other domestic sales, and international sales. Japan's Bridgestone Corporation, the world's third largest tire manufacturer, uses the global customer design in selling tires worldwide under its brand names Bridgestone and Firestone. One division deals with automobile manufacturers such as Ford, Nissan, and BMW, which buy tires as original equipment for new automobiles. Another division deals with individual consumers and market tires through the firm's network of automotive retail outlets. Still another division markets tires to agricultural users through firms such as Decree and Case.

This design is useful when various customer groups targeted by the firm are so diverse as to require totally distinct marketing approaches. For example, selling four replacement tires to an individual is a completely different task from selling 4 million tires to an automaker. The global customer approach allows the firm to meet the specific needs of each customer segment and track how well its products or services are doing among those segments. On the other hand, the global customer design results in a significant duplication of resources, since each customer group needs its own area and functional specialists. Coordination between the different divisions is also difficult, since each is concerned with a fundamentally different market.

Figure 1-18

Global Customer Design of NEC's Marketing Operation

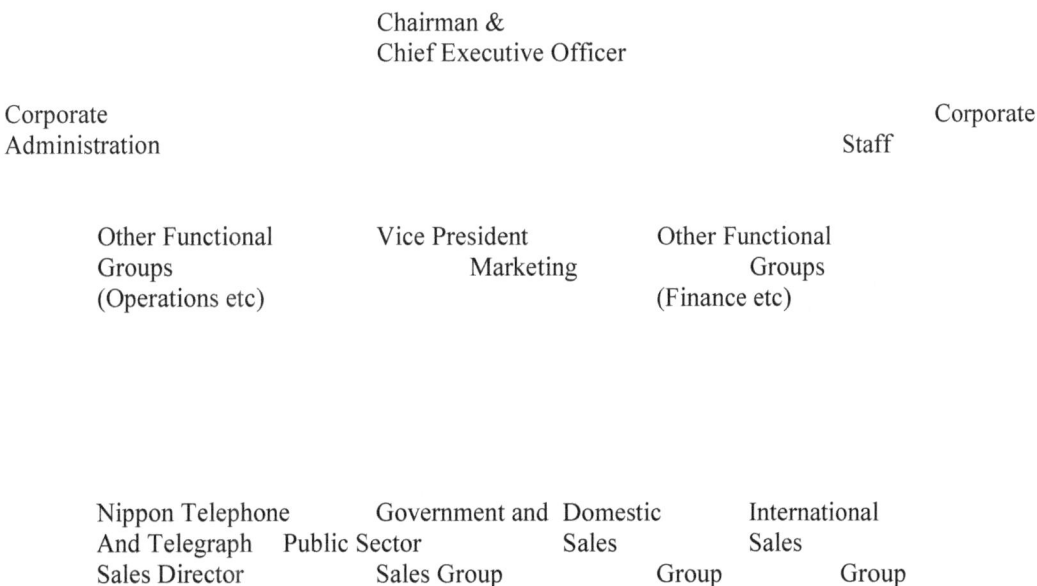

Chairman & Chief Executive Officer

Corporate Administration

Staff

Corporate

Other Functional Groups (Operations etc)

Vice President Marketing

Other Functional Groups (Finance etc)

Nippon Telephone And Telegraph Sales Director

Government and Public Sector Sales Group

Domestic Sales Group

International Sales Group

Global Matrix Design

The most complex form of international organization design is the global matrix design. A global matrix design is the result of superimposing one form of organization design on top of an existing, different form. The resulting design is usually quite fluid, with new matrix dimensions being created, downscaled, and eliminated as needed. For example, the global matrix design show in Figure 1-19 was created by superimposing a global product design. Using a global matrix design, a firm can form specific product groups comprising members from existing functional departments. These product groups can then plan, design, develop, produce, and market new products with appropriate input from each functional area. In this way, the firm can draw on both the functional and the product expertise of its employees. After a given product development task is completed, the product group may be dissolved; its members will then move on to new assignments. And, of course, other matrix arrangements are possible. For example an area design could be overload on a functional design, thereby allowing area specialists to coordinate activities with functional experts.

The global matrix design has the advantage of helping to bring together the functional area, and product expertises of the firm into teams that develop new products correspond to new challenges in the global marketplace. For example, Texas Instruments (TI) often uses a global matrix design is based on function. At any time, it has several product development groups in operation. Within any given country which TI operates, the groups draw members from relevant functional groups and work toward creating new products or new uses for existing ones.

When and if such breakthroughs are achieved, matrix-based product groups are used to transfer the new technology throughout the rest of the firm. After the task assigned to the product group is completed (for example, after the new product is launched), the group may be dissolved.

The global matrix design thus promotes organizational flexibility. It allows firms to take advantage of functional area, customer, and product organization designs as needed while simultaneously minimizing the disadvantages of each. Members of a product development team can be added or dropped from the team as the firm's need change. The global matrix design also promotes coordination and communication among managers from different divisions.

The global matrix design has disadvantages, however:-
1. It is not appropriate for a firm that has few products and that operates in relatively stable markets.
2. It often puts employees in the position of being accountable to more than one manager. For example, at any given time an employee may be a member of his or her functional area, or product group as well as of two or three product development groups. As a result, the individual may have split loyalties, and often times caught between competing sets of demands and pressures as the area manager the employee reports to wants one thing and the product-line manager wants another.
3. The global matrix design creates a paradox regarding authority. On the one hand, part of its purpose is to put decision-making authority in the hands of those managers most able to use it quickly. On the other hand, because reporting relationships are so complex and vague, getting approval for major decisions may actually be slower.
4. It tends to promote compromises or decisions based on the relative political clout of the managers involved.

Hybrid Global Designs

A final point to consider is that each global form of international organization design described represents an ideal. Most firms create a hybrid design that best suits their purposes, as dictated in part by size, strategy, technology, environment, and culture. Most MNCs, in particular, are likely to blend elements of all these designs. A firm may use a basic product design as its overall approach, but it may have different levels of functional orientation or area focus in some of its product groups than in others. For instance, this is the approach used by Nestle. Special customer groups and specific markets may also have divisions or support groups that span all areas in a firm. In fact, if it were possible to compare the designs used by the world's largest MNCs, no two would look exactly the same. A firm's managers start with the basic prototype discussed here, merged them, throw out bits and pieces, and create new elements unique to their firm as they respond to changes in the organization's strategy and competitive environment.

Figure 1-20 illustrates how Nissan Motor Corporation uses a hybrid design to structure its U.S. operations. A the top level of the firm, Nissan has some managers dedicated to products (such as the vice president and general manager for the Infiniti division) and others dedicated to functions (such as the vice president and chief financial officer). The marketing function for Nissan automobiles is broken down by product, with specific units responsible for sedans, sports cars, and trucks and utility vehicles. Both the Infiniti and Nissan divisions also have regional general managers organized by area.

In a similar way, all large international organizations mix and match forms of organizations in different areas and at different levels to create hybrid organization designs that their managers believe best serve the firm's needs.

Figure 1-19

A Global Matrix Design

CEO

Global   Global   Global   Global
Marketing   Finance   Operations   HRM

Global Product
Manager A

Global Product
Manger B

Global Product
Manager C

Global Product
Manager D

Figure 1-20

Chairman & Chief Executive Officer

Vice   Vice   Manager Vice   Vice   Vice
President   President   Office of   President   President   President
& General   & General   Corp   General Corporate   Chief
Manager Manager Comm.   Counsel Strategy Financial
Infiniti   Operations   Resource   Officer
Division Support Grp   Dev

General Manager   Vice President & Manager Manager
Marketing   Parts/Services   General Manager Office of   Information
Manager Marketing   Nissan Division Corporate   Services
                                                     Human
                                                     Resources

Manager Manager General Regional   General
Advertising   Parts / Supply Manager General   Auditor
          Distribution   Operations   Managers   Manager
                                                     Office of
General Manager   General   Corporate   Manager
Sales   Consumer   Marketing   Training Financial
Manager Affairs   Manager   Analysis /
                                                              Planning
                                                     Manager

Manager Manager Manager Manager Corporate

Staff   Vehicle Sedan   Truck /   Strategy &   Controller
Operations   Logistics   Marketing   Utility   Planning
                                    Marketing
                                                  EVP
Regional   Manager Manager Manager Operations
General Production   Sports Car   Marketing   NFTI
Managers   Engineering   Marketing   Communications
East   Support
Central
& West

             Manager
             Field
             Technician
             Support

Chapter Three

Crossing Border For Cross Cultural Management

Motivation in International Business

All international businesses encounter the challenge of motivating their work forces to reduce costs, develop new products, enhance product quality, and improve customer service. Yet most managers know that the factors that influence an individual's behavior at work differ across cultures. An appreciation of these individual differences is an important first step in understanding how managers can better understand, assess and address behavioral and interpersonal processes in different cultures.

Motivation

Motivation is the overall set of forces that cause people to choose certain behaviors from a set of available behaviors. Most modern theoretical approaches to motivation fall into one of the three categories:
1. Need-based models of motivation, which attempt to identify the specific needs or set of needs that result in motivated behavior.
2. Process-based models of motivation, which focus more on the conscious thought processes people use to select one behavior from among several.
3. The reinforcement model of motivation, which deals with how people assess the consequences of their behavioral choices and how that assessment affects the future choice of behaviors and incorporates the roles of rewards and punishment in maintaining or altering existing behavioral patterns.

Given the different set of orientations of national cultures explored by Hofstede and others, an international manager believes that the factors motivating Japanese, Mexican, or Chinese workers differ fundamentally from those found to be important in the United States. That manager would be right.

Need-Based Models Across Cultures

Hofstede's work provides some useful insights into how need-based models of motivation are likely to vary across cultures. The common needs incorporated in most models of motivation include the needs for security, for being part of a social network, and for opportunities to grow and develop. By relating these need categories to Hofstede's original four dimensions, social orientation, power orientation, uncertainty orientation, and goal orientation, several inferences can be drawn about differences in motivation across cultures.

For example, managers and employees in countries that are individualistic may be most strongly motivated by individually based needs and rewards. Opportunities to demonstrate personal competencies and to receive recognition and rewards as a result may be particularly attractive to such people. In contrast, people from collectivistics cultures may be more strongly motivated by group-based needs and rewards. Indeed, they may be uncomfortable in situations in which they are singled out for rewards apart from the group with which they work.

Conflicts can result when an international firm's mechanisms for motivating workers clash with cultures attitudes. For example, many U.S. managers working for Japanese MNCs have difficulty with the seniority-based, group performance-oriented compensation systems of their employers. Similarly, Michigan autoworkers resisted the attempts by Mazda officials to get them to "voluntarily" wear Mazda baseball caps as part of their work uniforms. Tom Selleck's movie, Mr Baseball illustrated still other aspects of the cultural clashes arising from these motivational differences between the individual oriented U.S. culture and the group-oriented Japanese culture. Especially, U.S. baseball players, accustomed to the "Star System" that accords them status, prestige, and special privileges, are often surprised by the team-based approach in Japan, which discourages attention to individuals.

Power-respecting individuals are those who accept their boss's right to direct their efforts purely on the basis of organizational legitimacy. As a result of this power respect they may be motivated by the possibility of gaining their boss's approval and acceptances. Thus they may willingly and unquestioningly accept and attempt to carry out directives and mandates. In contrast, power-tolerant people attract less legitimacy to hierarchical rank. Thus they may be less motivated by gaining their boss's approval than by opportunities for pay raises and promotions.

Managers and employees in uncertainty-avoiding cultures may be highly motivate by opportunities to maintain or increase their perceived levels of job security and job stability. Any effort to reduce or eliminate that security or stability may be met with resistance. In contrast, people in uncertainty-accepting cultures may be less motivated by security needs and less inclined to seek job security or stability as a condition of employment. They also may be more motivated by change and by new challenges and opportunities for personal growth and development. For example, a research comparing U.S. and German workers reveal substantial differences in their preferences regarding job values. Job security and shorter work hours were valued more highly by the German workers than the U.S. workers. Income, opportunities for promotion, and the importance of one's work were much more highly valued by the U.S. workers than by their German counterparts.

Finally, people from more aggressive goal behavior cultures are more likely to be motivated by money and other material rewards. They may pursue behavioral choices that they perceive as having the highest probability of financial payoff. They also may be disinclined to work toward reward whose primary attraction is mere comfort or personal satisfaction. In contrast, workers in a passive goal behavior cultures may be more motivated by needs and rewards that can potentially enhance the quality of their lives. They may be less interested in behavioral choices whose primary appeal is a higher financial payoff. For example, Swedish firms provide generous vacations and fringe benefits, while firms operating in China, where wage rates are low by world standards, normally provide workers with housing, medical care, and other support services.

Various researchers have tested specific motivation theories in different cultural settings. The theory receiving the most attention has been Abraham Maslow's hierarchy of five basic needs, physiological, security, social, self-esteem, and self-actualization. International research on Maslow's hierarchy provides two different insights. First, managers in many different countries, including the United States, Mexico, Japan and Canada, usually agree that the needs included in Maslow's hierarchy are all important to them. Second, the relative importance and preference ordering of the needs vary considerably by country. For example, managers in less developed countries such as Liberia and India plan a higher priority on satisfying self-esteem and security needs than do managers from more developed countries.

Results from research based on another motivation theory, David McClelland's learned needs framework, have been slightly more consistent. In particular, the need for achievement (to grow, learn, and accomplish important things) has been shown to exist in many different countries. McClelland has also demonstrated that the need for achievement can be taught to people in different cultures. However, given the role of Hofstede's cultural differences, it follows that Mcclelland's needs are not likely to be constant across cultures. In particular, individualistic, uncertainty-accepting, power-tolerant, and aggressive goal behavior cultures seem most likely to foster and promote the needs for achievement and power (to control resources) but not the need for affiliation (to be part of a social network). In contrast, collectivistic, uncertainty-avoiding, power-respecting, and passive goal behavior cultures may promote the need for affiliation more than the needs for achievement and power.

Federick Herzberg's two-factor theory is another popular need-based theory of motivation. This theory suggests that one set of factors affects dissatisfaction and another set affects satisfaction. It too, has been tested cross-culturally with varied results. For example, research has found different patterns of factors when comparing U.S. managers with managers from New Zealand and Panama. Results from U.S. employees suggested that supervision contributed to dissatisfaction but not to satisfaction. But supervision did contribute to employers' satisfaction in New Zealand. Panama is at Southern part of U.S. therefore have a different culture as the Northern Americans. Hence inconsistent results within a same country. The theory is well known and popular among managers.

Process-Based Models Across Cultures

In contrast to need-based theories, expectancy theory takes a process view of motivation. The theory suggests that people are motivated to behave in certain ways to the extent that they perceive that such behaviors will lead to outcomes they find personally attractive. The theory acknowledges that different people have different needs, one person may need money, another recognition, another social satisfaction , and still another prestige. But each will be willing to improve his or her performance if he or she believes the result will be fulfilment of the needs he or she most prefers.

Though there has been relatively little research that explicitly tests expectancy theory in countries other than the United States. It does seem logical, however, that the basic framework of the theory should have wide applicability. Regardless of where people work, they are likely to work toward goals they think are important. However, cultural factors will partially determine both the nature of those work goals and peoples' perceptions of how they should most fruitfully pursue them.

One salient complex factor that is likely to affect the expectancy process is the cultural dimension of social orientation. The expectancy theory is essentially a model of individual decision regarding individual behavioral choices targeted at individual outcomes. Thus it may be difficult to explain behavior in collectivistic cultures, but otherwise may be one of the most likely candidates for a culturally unbiased explanation of motivated behavior. For example, the expectancy theory helps explain the success story Sony has enjoyed. Employees who work for Sony know they will be able to pursue diverse opportunities and will be kept informed about what is happening in the firm. People who see these conditions as especially important will be most strongly motivated to work for Sony.

The Reinforcement Model across Cultures

Like the expectancy theory, the reinforcement model has undergone relatively few tests in different cultures. Basically, this model says that behavior that results in a positive outcome (reinforcement) will be likely to be repeated under the same circumstances in the future. Behavioral choice that results in negative consequences (punishment) will result in a different choice under the same circumstance in the future. As this model makes no attempt to specify what people will find reinforcing or punishing, it may also be generalizable to different cultures.

Like the expectancy theory, the reinforcement model has exceptions. In Muslim cultures, for example, people tend to believe that the consequences they experience are the will of God rather than a function of their own behavior. Thus neither reinforcement nor punishment will have much effort on their future behavioral decisions. Aside from relatively narrow exceptions such as this, however, the reinforcement model, like the expectancy theory, warrants careful attention from international managers, provided they understand what constitutes rewards and punishment will vary across cultures.

Cultural Dimensions of International Management

Basic Perspectives on Individual Differences

The term individual differences refer to specific dimensions or characteristics of a person that influence that person's perceptions, attitudes, values, or behaviors. Psychologists who study individual differences focus primarily on personality traits and need structures. However, these factors are influenced by the culture in which a person grew up. International business managers, who face the challenge of managing and motivating employees with different cultural backgrounds, need to understand what these personality traits and need structures are and how they differ across cultures. Fortunately, an increasing number of studies by industrial psychologists and organizational behavior specialists are identifying these cultural differences, thereby helping international business managers manage the people more effectively.

One of the most influential of these studies is that of Geert Hofstede, a Dutch researcher who studied 116,000 people working in dozens of different countries. (though Hofstede's research has been criticized for methodological weaknesses and his own cultural biases, however remains the largest and most comprehensive work of its kind). Hofstede's initial work identified four important dimensions along which people seem to differ across cultures. However recently, he added a fifth dimension. These dimensions, are illustrated in Figure 1-20 are as follows:-
1. Social Orientation
2. Power Orientation
3. Uncertainty Orientation
4. Goal Orientation
5. Time Orientation

Observations were made that these dimensions do not represent absolutes, but instead reflect tenderness within cultures. Within any given culture, there are likely to be people at every point on each dimension.

Social Orientation

The first dimension identified by Hofstede is social orientation (I have altered Hofstede's terminology a bit for the sake of clarity). Social orientation is a person's beliefs about the relative importance of the individual and the groups to which that person belongs. The two extremes of social orientation, summarized in Table 1-5, are individualism and collectivism. Individualism is the cultural belief that the person comes first. People who hold this belief tend to put their own interests and those of their immediate families ahead of those of others. Key values of individualistic people include a high degree of self-respect and independence but a corresponding lack of tolerance for opposing viewpoints. These people often put their own success through competition over the good of the group, and they tend to assess decisions in terms of how those decisions affect them as individuals. Hofstede's research suggested that people in the United States, the United Kingdom, Australia, Canada, New Zealand, and the Netherlands tend to be relatively individualistic.

Collectivism

Collectivism, the opposite of individualism, is the belief that the group comes first. Societies that tend to be collectivistic are usually characterized by well-defined social networks, including extended families, tribes, and co-workers. People are expected to put the good of the group ahead of their own personal freedom, interests, or success. Individual behavior in such cultures is strongly influenced by the emotion of shame; when a group fails, its members take that failure very personally and experience shame. In addition, group members try to fit into their group harmoniously, with a minimum of conflict or tension. Hofstede found that people from Mexico, Greece, Hongkong, Taiwan, Peru, Singapore, Colombia, and Pakistan tend to be relatively collectivistic in their values.

International firms must be aware of differences in the cultural orientations of countries among the social orientation dimension. In countries such as the United states, where individualism is a cultural norm, many workers prefer reward system that link pay with individual performance. In a more collectivistic culture such as China prior to the implementation of its economic reforms, such a reward system may, in fact, be counter productive. For example, Beijing Jeep once promoted a productive and promising young employee, granting him a raise of $2.70 a month (a 5 percent increase) for his efforts. However, the employee found this 5 percent raise a mixed blessing after his co-workers began to shun him. The raise violated China's collectivistic norms.

A similar pattern characterizes the career progression of employees. In individualistic societies, a person's career path often involves switching employees in a search for higher-paying and more challenging jobs so that the person can prove his or her capabilities in new and changing circumstances. But in collectivistic cultures, even those that are only moderately so, such as Japan, a person's changing jobs reflects disloyalty to the collective good (the firm) and may brand the person a unworthy of trust. Similarly, nepotism is often frowned on in individualistic cultures but may be a normal hiring practice in collectivistic ones.

Power Orientation

The second dimension Hofstede proposed is power orientation refers to the beliefs that people in a culture hold about the appropriateness of power and authority differences in hierarchies such as business organizations. The extremes of the dimension of power orientation are summarized in Table 1-6.

Some cultures are characterized by power respect. This means that people in a culture tend to accept the power and authority of their superiors simply on the basis of the superiors' positions in the hierarchy and to respect the superiors' right to that power. People at all levels in a firm accept the decisions and mandates of those above them because of their implicit belief that those higher-level positions carry with them the right to make those decisions and issue those mandates. Hofstede found people in France, Spain, Mexico, Japan, Brazil, Indonesia, and Singapore to be relatively power respecting.

In contrast, people in cultures characterized by power tolerance attach much less significance to a person's position in the hierarchy. Those people are more willing to question a decision or mandate from someone at a higher level or perhaps even refuse to accept it. They are willing to follow a leader when that leader is perceived to be right or when it seems to be in their own self-interest to do so, but not because of the leader's intangible right to issue orders. Hofstede's work suggested that people in the United States, Israel, Austria, Denmark, Ireland, Norway, Germany, and New Zealand tend to be more power tolerant.

Differing cultural attitudes toward power orientation can lead to misunderstandings in business. For example, when firms are negotiating with each other, a firm from a power-tolerant country will often send a team composed of experts on the subject, without concern for rank or seniority. But a team composed of junior employees, no matter how knowledgeable they are about the problem at hand, will be taken as an insult by managers from power-respecting cultures, who expect to deal with persons of rank equal to their own. Also, the quick adoption of informalities by U.S. managers, for example, calling a counterpart by that person's first name, may be misinterpreted by managers from power respecting cultures as an insulting attempt to diminish another's authority.

Similarly, the willingness of a U.S. manager to roll up his or her sleeves and pitch in on the factory floor in an emergency is likely to win praise from U.S. production workers. In Kenya, a superior who exhibit such behavior would be demonstrating his contempt for the management role. A manager so lacking in self-respect would be deemed unworthy of respect or obedience from Kenyan workers. A different perspective on Hofstede's dimensions by viewing them in combinations. For example, when social orientation and power orientation are superimposed, individualistic and power-tolerant countries seem to cluster, as do collectivistic and power-respecting countries.

Figure 1-20

INDIVIDUALISM The Interest of the individual take **precedence**	**SOCIAL ORIENTATION** Relative importance of the interests of the individual **vs the interests of the group**	**COLLECTIVISM** The interests of the group take precedence
POWER RESPECT Authority is inherent in one's position within a hierarchy	*POWER ORIENTATION* The appropriateness of power/authority within organization	*POWER TOLERANCE* Individuals assess authority in view of its perceived rightness or their own personal interests.
UNCERTAINTY **ACCEPTANCE** Positive response to change and new opportunities	**UNCERTAINTY** **ORIENTATION** An emotional response to uncertainty and change	**UNCERTAINTY** **AVOIDANCE** Prefer structure and a consistent routine
AGGRESSIVE GOAL **BEHAVIOR** Value material possessions, money, and assertiveness	**GOAL ORIENTATION** What motivates people to achieve different goals	**PASSIVE GOAL** **BEHAVIOR** Value social relevance quality of life, and the welfare of others
LONG-TERM **OUTLOOK** Value dedication, hardwork, and self-image	TIME ORIENTATION The extent to which members of a culture adopt a long-term or a short-term outlook on work and life	SHOT-TERM **OUTLOOK** Place less emphasis on hard work

Table 1-5

Extremes of Social Orientation

ENVIRONMENT	COLLECTIVISM	INDIVIDUALISM
In the family	Education toward "we" Consciousness Opinions predetermined by Group. Obligations to family or in group :- 1. Harmony 2. Respect 3. Shame	Education toward "I" consciousness Private Opinion expected. Obligations to self: 1. Self-interest 2. Self-actualization 3. Guilt
At School	Learning is for the young only Learn how to do	Continuing education Learn how to learn
At the workplace	Value standards differ for in-group and out-groups: particularlism Other people seem as members of their group Relationship prevails over task moral model of employer-employee relationship	Same value standards apply to all: universalism Other people seem as potential resources Task prevails over relationship Calculative model of employer Employee Relationship

Table 1-6

Extremes of Power Orientation

ENVIRONMENT	*POWER TOLERANCE*	*POWER RESPECT*
In the Family	Children encouraged to have a will of their own parents treated as equals	Children educated toward obedience to parents. Parents treated as superiors
At School	Student-centered education (initiative) learning represents impersonal "truth"	Teacher-centered education (order) learning represents personal "wisdom" from teacher (guru)
At Workplace	Hierarchy means an inequality of roles, established for convenience subordinates expect to be consulted	Hierarchy means existential inequality subordinates expect to be told what to do, ideal boss is benevolent autocrate (good father)

Uncertainty Orientation

The third basic dimension of individual differences Hofstede studied is uncertainty orientation. Uncertainty orientation is the feeling people have regarding uncertain and ambiguous situations. The extremes of this dimension are illustrated in Table 1-7.

People in cultures characterized by uncertainty acceptance are stimulated by change and thrive on new opportunities. Ambiguity is seen as a context within which an individual can grow, develop, and carve out new opportunities. In these cultures, certainty carries with it a sense of monotony, routineness, and overbearing structure. Hofstede suggested that many people from the United states, Denmark, Sweden, Canada, Singapore, Hongkong, and Australia are uncertainty accepting.

In contrast, people in cultures characterized by uncertainty avoidance dislike and will avoid ambiguity whenever possible. Ambiguity and change are seen as undesirable. These people tend to prefer a structured and routine, even bureaucratic, way of doing things. Hofstede found that many people in Israel, Austria, Japan, Italy, Columbia, France, Peru and Germany tend to avoid uncertainty.

Uncertainty orientation affects many aspects of managing international firms. Those operating in uncertainty – avoiding countries, for example, tend to adopt more rigid hierarchies and more elaborate rules and procedures for doing business. Uncertainty-accepting cultures, on the other hand, are more tolerant of flexible hierarchies, rules, and procedures. Risk taking ("nothing ventured, nothing gained") is highly valued in uncertainty-accepting countries such as the United States and Hong Kong, whereas preserving the statues and prestige of the firm through conservative, low risk strategies is more important in uncertainty-avoiding countries such as Spain, Belgium, and Argentina.

It is interesting to consider uncertainty orientation along with the social orientation dimension. For example, job mobility is likely to be higher in uncertainty-accepting countries then in those characterized by uncertainty avoidance. Some Japanese firms have traditionally used lifetime employment practices partly in response to the uncertainty-avoiding and collectivistic tendencies of the Japanese culture.

Yet lifetime employment – as well as seniority-based pay and promotion policies used by Japanese firms, may not be an effective policy when transplanted to individualistic an uncertainty-accepting countries. For example, Japanese firms operating in uncertainty-accepting Canada and the United States have been forced to modify their pay and promotion policies because North American workers are more oriented toward an individualistic "pay me what I'm worth" attitude and are less worried about job security than are their counterparts in Japan.

Table 1-7

Extremes of Uncertainty Orientation

Environment	Uncertainty Acceptance	Uncertainty Avoidances
In the Family	What is different is ridiculous or curious ease, indolence, low stress aggression and emotions not shown	What is different is dangerous Higher anxiety and stress Showing of aggression and emotions accepted
At School	Students comfortable with - Unstructured learning situation - Vague Objective - Broad assignments - No timetables Teachers may say "I don't know"	Students comfortable with - Structured learning situation - Precise objective - Detailed assignments - Strict timetables Teachers should have all the Answers

At the Workplace Dislike of rules, written or
              unwritten
              less formalization and
              standardization

              Emotional need for rules,
              written or unwritten
              More formalization and
              Standardization

Goal Orientation

The fourth dimension of cultural values Hofstede measured is goal orientation. In this context, goal orientation is the manner in which people are motivated to work toward different kinds of goals. One extreme on the goal orientation continuum is aggressive goal behavior. (See Table 1-8). People who exhibit aggressive goal behavior tend to place a high premium on material possessions, money, and assertiveness. At the other extreme, people who adopt passive goal behavior place a higher value on social relationships., quality of life, and concern for others.

According to Hofstede, cultures that value aggressive goal behavior also tend to define gender-based roles somewhat rigidly, whereas cultures that emphasize passive goal behavior do not. For example, in cultures characterized by extremely aggressive goal behavior, men are expected to work and to focus their careers in traditionally male occupations; Women are generally expected not to work outside he home and to focus more on their families. If they do work outside the home, they are usually expected to pursue work in areas traditionally dominated by women. According to Hofstede' s research, many people in Japan tend to exhibit relatively aggressive goal behavior, whereas many people in Germany, Mexico, Italy and the Untied States exhibit moderately aggressive goal behavior. Men and women in passive goal behavior cultures are more likely both to pursue diverse careers and to be well represented within any given occupation. People from the Netherlands, Norway, Sweden, Denmark, and Finland tend to exhibit relatively passive goal behavior.

These cultural attitudes affect international business practices in many ways. For example, one study showed that decisions made by Danish managers (a passive goal behavior culture) incorporate societal concerns to a greater extent than those made by more profit-oriented U.S, British, and German executives (from more aggressive goal behavior cultures). Similarly studies of the Swedish workforce indicate that country's egalitarian traditions, as well as workers' desires to maintain a comfortable work schedule, often make promotions less desirable than in other countries.

The Swedish tax code, which until recently taxed higher-income workers with marginal tax rates of 97 percent, reinforced this cultural norm by diminishing the value of any pay raise that accompanied a promotion. Many Swedish workers prefer more fringe benefits rather than higher salaries. Or consider the impact of the role of women in business. In Sweden, the high proportion of dual-career families makes it difficult for many workers to accept a promotion if it entails moving. And, not surprisingly, Swedish firms are among the world's leaders in providing fringe benefits such as maternity and paternity leave and company-sponsored child care.

Differences in goal orientation also affect production techniques. For example, Volvo sought to maintain its product quality and competitiveness by pioneering the use of flexible work groups to produce automobiles. This technique is a means of promoting job satisfaction and reflect Sweden's passive goal behavior, as well as its uncertainty acceptance. Japanese manufacturers, on the other hand, developed quality circles. This practice, inaugurated to promote quality, mirrors the more aggressive goal behavior and the collectivistic aspects of Japanese culture.

Time Orientation

Hofstede recently introduced a fifth dimension into his framework. This dimension, called time orientation, is the extent to which members of a culture adopt a long-term versus a short-term outlook on work, life, and other aspects of society.

Some cultures, such as those of Japan, Hong Kong, Taiwan, and South Korea, have a long-term orientation that values dedication, hard work, perseverance, and the importance of self-image. Other cultures, including Pakistan and West Africa, are more likely to have a short-term orientation. These cultures put considerably less emphasis on work, perseverance, and similar values. Hofstede's work suggests that the United States and Germany tend to have an intermediate time orientation.

Table 1-8

Extremes Of Goal Orientation

Environment	Passive Goal Behavior	Aggressive Goal Behavior
In the Family	Stress on relationships solidarity resolution of conflicts by compromise and negotiation	Stress on achievement competition resolution of conflicts by fighting them out
At School	Average student is norm system rewards students' social adaptation student's failure at school is relatively minor problem	Best students are norm system rewards students' academic performance student's failure at school is disaster; may lead to suicide.
At the Workplace	Assertiveness ridiculed undersell yourself stress on life quality intuition	Assertiveness appreciated overall yourself stress on careers decisiveness

Intercultural Communications and Understanding the Cultural Process

Cultural communications are more profound and more complex than spoken or written messages. The essence of effective cross-cultural communication has more to do with releasing the right responses than with sending the "right" messages.

The term communication describes the process of sharing meaning by transmitting messages through media such as words, behavior, or material artifacts. International managers communicate to coordinate activities, to disseminate information, to motivate people, and to negotiate future plans. It is of utmost importance, then, that the meaning of a particular communication is interpreted by the receiver the way it is intended by the sender. Unfortunately, the communication process, as illustrated in Exhibit 1-2, involves stages during which the meaning can be distorted. Anything that serves to undermine the communication of the intended meaning is typically referred to as noise.

The primary cause of noise is the fact that the sender and the receiver each exists in a unique, private world called his or her life space. The context of that private world, based largely on culture, experiences, relationships, values, and so on and so forth, determines the interpretation of meaning in communication. People filter, or selectively understand, messages according to what is consistent with their own expectations and perceptions of reality and their values and norms of behavior. The more dissimilar the cultures of those involved, the more likely there will be misinterpretation. In this way, different nations having different cultural backgrounds pervade the communication process.

Culture not only dictates who talks with whom, about what, and how the communication proceeds, it also helps to determine how people encode messages, the meanings they have for messages, and the conditions and circumstances under which various messages may or may not be sent, noticed, or interpreted. In fact, our entire repertory of communicative behaviors is dependent largely on the culture in which we have been raised. Culture, consequently, is the foundation of communication. And, when cultures vary, communication practices also vary.

Communications, therefore, is a complex process of linking up or sharing the perceptual fields of sender and receiver; the perceptive sender builds a bridge to the life space of the receiver. After the receiver interprets the message and draws a conclusion about what the sender meant, he or she will, in most cases, encode and sent back a response, making communication a circular process.

Exhibit 1-2

The Communication Process

Sender	Medium	Receiver
Meaning Encode	Message	Decode meaning

NOISE

CULTURE

FEED BACK

Cultural Noise in the Communication Process

Because our focus here is on effective cross-cultural communication, we need to understand what cultural variables cause noise in the communication process. This knowledge of cultural noise will enable us to take steps to minimize that noise and so improve communication.

When a member of one culture sends a message to a member of another culture, intercultural communication takes place. The message contains the meaning intended by the encoder. When it reaches the receiver, however, it undergoes a transformation in which the influence of the decoder's culture becomes part of the meaning. Exhibit 1-3 illustrates an example of intercultural communication in which the meaning got all mixed up. Note how the attribution of behavior differs for each participant. Attribution is the process in which people look for the explanation of another person's behavior. When they realize that they do not understand each other, they tend, say Hall and Hall, but blame it on the other person's silliness.

In the circumstances depicted in Exhibit 1-3, the Greek employee gets frustrated and resigns after communication problems with his American boss. How could this outcome have been avoided? The information about the people or the context of the situation is not available, but we can look at some of the variables these might have been involved and use them as a basis for analysis.

Cultural Variables in the Communication Process

Cultural variables that can affect the communication process by influencing a person's perceptions have been identified by Samovar and Portar and discussed by Harris and Moran, Ronen, and others. These variables are as follows:-
1. Attributes
2. Social organization
3. Thought patterns,
4. Roles,
5. Language (spoken or written),
6. Nonverbal communication (including Kinesia behavior, proxemics, paralanguage and object language), and
7. Time

Although these variables are separately discussed, their effects are interdependent and inseparable, or, as Hecht, Anderson, and Ribeau put it "Encoders and decoders process non-verbal cues as a conceptual, multi-channeled gestalt.

Attitudes

We all realized that our attitudes underlie the way we behave and communicate and the way we interpret messages from other people. Ethno-centric attitudes are a particular source of noise in cross-cultural communication. In the incident described in Exhibit 1-3, both the American and the Greek are clearly attempting to interpret and convey meaning based on their own experiences of that kind of transaction. The American is probably guilty of stereotyping the Greek employee by quickly jumping to the conclusion that he is unwilling to take responsibility for the task and the scheduling.

This problem, stereotyping, occurs when a person assumes that every member of a society or subculture has the same characteristics or traits. Stereotyping is a common cause of misunderstanding in intercultural communication. It is an arbitary, lazy, and often destructive way to find out about people. A stereotype should be distinguished from a sociotype, a means of accurately describing members of a group by their traits, which is useful to provide some initial basis for understanding people in a new encounter. Astute international managers are aware of the dangers of cultural stereotyping and deal with each person as an individual with whom they may form a unique relationship.

Social organizations

Our perception can be influenced by differences in values, approach, or priorities relative to the kind of social organizations to which we belong. These organizations may be based on one's nation, tribe, or religious sect, or they may consist of the members of a certain profession – example of such organizations include the Academy of Management or the UAW (United Auto Workers).

Exhibit 1-3

Cultural Noise in International Communication

Country	Behavior	Attribution
American:	"How long will it take you to finish this report ?"	American : I asked him to participate Greek : His behavior makes no sense He is the boss. Why doesn't he tell Me ??
Greek:	"I don't know. How long should it take ?"	American: He refuses to take responsibility. Greek : I asked him for an order.
American :	"You are in the best position to analyze time requirements."	American: I press him to take responsibility for his actions. Greek: What nonsense. I'd better give him an answer.
Greek ;	"10 days."	American: He lacks the ability to estimate time; this time estimate is totally inadequate.
American:	"Take 15. Is it agreed? You will do it in 15 days"	American: I offer a contract Greek: These are my orders: 15 days.

In fact, the report needed 30 days of regular work. So the Greek worked day and night, but at the end of the 15th day, he still needed to do one more day's work.

American:	"Where is the report?"	American: I am making sure he fulfills his contract.

		Greek: He is asking for the report.
Greek:	"It will be ready tomorrow"	(Both attribute that it is not ready)
American:	"But we agreed it would be ready today."	American: I must teach him to fulfill a contract. Greek: The stupid, incompetent boss! Not only did he give me the wrong orders, but he doesn't even appreciate that I did a 30-day job In 16 days.
The Greek hands in his resignation.		The American is surprised. Greek: I can't work for such a man.

Thought Patterns

The logical progression of reasoning varies widely around the world and greatly affects the communication process. Managers cannot assume that others use the same reasoning processes, as illustrated by the experience of a Canadian expatriate in Thailand.

While in Thailand, a Canadian expatriate's car was hit by a Thai motorist who had crossed over the double line while passing another vehicle. After failing to establish that the fault lay with the Thai driver, the Canadian flagged down a policeman. After several minutes of seemingly futile discussion, the Canadian pointed out the double line in the middle of the road and asked the policeman directly, "What do these lines signify?" The policeman replied, "They indicate the center of the road and are there so I can establish just how far the accident is from that point." The Canadian was silent. It had never occurred to him that the double line might not mean "no passing allowed."

In the Exhibit 1-3 scenario, perhaps the American did not realize that the Greek employee had a different rationale for his time estimate for the job. Because the Greek was not used to having to estimate schedules, he just took a guess, which he felt forced into.

Roles

Societies differ considerably in their perception of a manager's role. Much of the difference is attributable to their perception of who should make the decisions and who has responsibility for what. In the example, the American assumes that his role as manager is to delegate responsibility, to foster autonomy, and to practice participative management. He is prescribing the role of the employee without any consideration of whether the employee will understand that role. The Greek's frame of reference leads him to think that he manager is the boss and should give the order about when to have the job completed. He interprets the American's behavior as breaking that frame of reference, and therefore he feels that the boss is "stupid and incompetent" for giving him the wrong order, and for not recognizing and appreciating his accomplishment. The manager should have considered what behaviors Greek workers would expect of him and then either played that role or discussed the situation carefully, in a training mode.

Language

Spoken or written language, of course, is a frequent cause of miscommunication, stemming from a person's inability to speak the local language, a poor or too-literal translation, a speaker's failure to explain idioms, or a person missing the meaning conveyed through body language or certain symbols. Even among countries that share the same language, there can be problems in the subtleties and nuances inherent in the use of the language, as noted by George Bernard Shaw: Britain and America are two nations separated by a common language. "This problem can exist even within the same country among subcultures or subgroups."
Many international executives tell stories about lost business deals or lost sales because of communication blunders.

When Pepsi Cola's slogan "Come Alive with Pepsi" was introduced in Germany, the company learned that the literal German translation of "Come Alive" is come out of the grave.

A U.S airline found a lack of demand for its "rendezvous lounges" on its Boeing 747s. They later learned that "rendezvous" in Portuguese refers to a room that is rented for prostitution.

More than just conveying objective information, language also conveys cultural and social understanding from one generation to the next. Examples of how language reflects what is important in a society include the 6,000 different Arabic words used to describe camels and their parts and the 50 or more classifications of snow used by the Inuit Eskimos.

In as much as language conveys culture, technology, and priorities, it also serves to separate and perpetuate subcultures. In India, 14 officials and many unofficial languages are use, and over 800 languages are spoken on the African continent.

Because of increasing workforce diversity around the world, the international business manager will have to deal with a medley of languages. For example, assembly-line workers at the Ford plant in Cologne speak Turkish and Spanish as well as German. In Malaysia, Indonesia, and Thailand, many of the buyers and traders are Chinese. Not all Arabs speak Arabic, in Tunisia and Lebanon, for example, French is the commercial language.

International managers need either a good command of the local language or competent interpreters. The task of accurate translation to bridge cultural gaps is fraught with difficulties, as Schermerhorn discovered in his study of 153 Hongkong Chinese bilinguals; he found a considerably difference in interpretation and response according to whether the medium used was Chinese or English, even after many experts were involved in the translation process.

Even the direct translation of specific words does not guarantee the congruence of their meaning, as with the word ""yes" used by Asians, which usually means only that they have heard you.

Politeness and a desire to say only what the listener wants to hear creates noise in the communication process in much of the world. Often, even a clear translation does not help a person to understand what is meant because the encoding process has obscured the true messages. With the poetic Arab language replete with exaggeration, elaboration, and repetition, meaning is attributed more to how something is said rather than what is said.

In exhibit 1-3, On the American supervisor and Greek employee, it is highly likely that the American could have picked up some cues from the employee from his body language, which probably implied problems with the interpretation of meaning.

Nonverbal Communication

Behavior that communicates without words (although it often is accompanied by words) is called nonverbal communication, or body language. People will usually believe what they see over what they hear hence the expression, "a picture is worth a thousand words." Studies show that these subtle messages account for between 65 and 93 percent of interpreted communication. The media for such nonverbal communication can be categorized into four types:-
1. Kinesic behavior
2. Proxemics
3. Paralanguage, and
4. Object language

The term Kinesic behavior refers to body movements, - posture, gestures, facial expression, and eye contact. While such actions may be universal, their meaning often is not. Because Kinesic systems of meaning are culturally specific and learned, they cannot be generalized across cultures. Most people in the West would not correctly interpret many Chinese facial expressions; sticking out the tongue expresses surprises, a widening of the eye shows anger, and scratch the ears and cheeks indicates happiness. Research has review for sometime, however, that most people worldwide can recognize displays of the basic emotions of anger, disgust, fear, happiness, sadness, surprise, and contempt.

Many business people and visitors react negatively to what they feel are inappropriate facial expressions, without understanding the cultural meaning behind them. In his studies of cross-cultural negotiations, Graham observed that the Japanese feel uncomfortable when faced with the Americans' eye to eye posture. They are taught since childhood to bow their heads out of humility, whereas the automatic response of Americans is "look at me when I'm talking to you."

Subtle differences in eye behavior (called ocutegics) can throw off a communication badly if they are not understood. Eye behavior includes differences not only in eye contact but also in the use of eyes to convey other messages, whether or not that involves mutual gaze. Edward T. Hall, author of the classic The Silent Language, explains the differences in eye contact between British and the Americans. During speaking the Americans will look straight at you, while the British keep your attention by looking away. They will then look at you when they have finished speaking, which signals that it is your turn to talk. The implicit rationale for this is that you can't interrupt people when they are not looking at you.

It is important for American managers to be aware of the many cultural expectations regarding posture and how they may be interpreted. In Europe or Asia, relaxed posture in business meetings may be taken as bad managers or the result of poor upbringing. In Korea you are expected to sit upright, with feet squarely on the floor, and to speak slowly, showing a blending of body and spirit.

International managers can also familiarize themselves with the many different interpretations of hand and finger signals around the world, some of which may even represent obscene gestures. Of course, we cannot expect to change all of our ingrained, natural Kinesics behavior, but we can be aware of what it means to others. And we can learn to understand the Kinesics behavior of others and the role it plays in their society, as well as how it can affect business transactions. Misunderstanding the meanings of body movements, or an ethnocentric attitude toward the "proper" behavior can have negative repercussions.

Polemics deals with the influence of proximity and space on communication both personal space and office space or layout. Americans expect office layout to provide private space for each person, usually a larger and more private space as one goes up the hierarchy. In many parts of Asia, the custom is open office space, with people at all levels working and talking in close proximity to one another. Space communicates power in both Germany and the United States, evidenced by the desire for a corner office or the top floor. The importance of French officials, however, is made clear by a position in the middle of subordinates, communicating that they have a central position in an information network, where they can stay informed and in control.

When someone feel vaguely uncomfortable and start slowly moving backward when another is speaking to them, is because that person is invading the "bubble" of his personal space. Personal space is culturally patterned, and foreign spatial aces are a common source of misinterpretation. When someone seems aloof or pushing, it often means that she or he is operating under subtly different spacial rules.

Hall and Hall suggest that cultural differences affect the programming of the senses and that space, perceived by all the senses, is regarded as a form of territory to be protected. South Americans, Southern and Eastern Europeans, Indonesians, and Arabs are high-contact cultures, preferring to stand close, touch a great deal, and experience a "close" sensory involvement. On the other hand, North Americans, Asians, and Northern Europeans are low-contact cultures and prefer much less sensory involvement, standing further apart and touching far less. They have a "distant" style of body language.

Interestingly, high-contact cultures are mostly located in warmer climates low-contact culture are in cooler climates. Americans are relatively non-touching, automatically standing at a distance so that an outstretched arm would touch the other person's ear. Standing any closer than that is treated as invading intimate space. However, Americans and Canadians certainly expect a warm handshake and maybe a pat on the back for closer friends, though not the very warm double handshake of the Spaniards (clasping the forearm with the left hand). The Japanese, considerably less haptic (touching), do not shake hands, an initial greeting between a Japanese and a Spanish business person would be uncomfortable for both parties if they were untrained in cultural haptics.

As we are considering high and low-contact cultures, we can trace a correlation between Hofstede's cultural variables of individualism and collectivism and the types of Kinesic and proxemic behaviors people display. Generally, people from individualistic cultures are more remote and distant, whereas those from collectivist cultures are interdependent, they tend to work, lay, live, and sleep in close proximity.

The term paralanguage refers to how something is said rather than the content, the rate of speech, the tone and inflection of voice, other noises, laughing or yawning. The culturally oriented manager learns how to interpret subtle differences in paralanguage, including silence. Silence is a powerful communicator. It may be a way of saying no, of being offended, or of waiting for more information to make a decision. Americans, very impatient with silence, don't know how to react. Graham, a researcher on international negotiations, taped a bargaining session held at Toyota's U.S. headquarters in California. The American executive had made a proposal to open a new production facility in Brazil and was waiting for a response from the three Japanese executives, who sat with lowered eyes and hands folded on the table. After about 30 seconds, an eternity to Americans, accustomed to a conversational response time of a few truths of a second, the American blurted out that they were getting nowhere, and the meeting ended in a statement. More sensitivity to cultural differences in communication might have led him to wait longer or perhaps to prompt some further response through another polite question.

The term object language, or material culture, refers to how we communicate through material artifacts, whether architecture, office design and furniture, clothing, cars or cosmetics. Material culture communicates what people hold as important. In Mexico, a visiting international executive or salesperson is advised to take time out, before negotiating business, to show appreciation for the surrounding architecture, which is prized by Mexicans.

Time

Another variable that communicates culture is the way people regard and use time. To Brazilians, relative punctuality communicates the level of importance of those involved. To middle Easterners, time is something controlled by the will of Allah.

To initiate effective cross-cultural business interactions, managers should know the difference between monochronic time systems and polychronic time systems and how they affect communications. Hall and Hall explain that in monochronic cultures (Switzerland, Germany, and the United States), time is experienced in a linear way, with a past, a present, and a future, and time is treated as something to be spent, saved, made-up, or wasted. Classified and compartmentalized, time serves to order life. This attitude, is a learned part of Western culture, probably starting with the industrial revolution. Monochronic people found in individualistic cultures, generally concentrate on one thing at a time, adhere to time commitments, and are accustomed to short term relationship.

In contrast, polychronic systems tolerate many things occurring simultaneously and emphasize involvement with people. Two Latin friends, for example, will put an important conversation a head of being on time for a business meeting, thus communicating the priority of relationships over material systems. Polychronic people, Latin Americans, Arabs, and those from other collectivist cultures may focus on several things at once, be highly distractible, and change plans often.

The relationship between time and space also affects communication. Polychronic people, for example, are likely to hold open meetings, moving around and conducting transactions from one party to another rather than compartmentalizing meeting topics, as do monochronic people.

Endless nuances and distinctions regarding cultural differences in nonverbal communications can be discussed. There are various forms illustrated in Exhibit 1-4, wise intercultural managers will take careful account of the role that such differences might play.

Exhibit 1-4

FORMS OF NONVERBAL COMMUNICATION

1. Hand gestures
2. Facial expressions, smiles, frowns, yawns
3. Posture and stance
4. Clothing hairstyles
5. Interpersonal distance (proxemics)
6. Touching
7. Eye contact and direction of graze, particularly in listening behavior
8. Architecture and interior design
9. Artifacts and nonverbal symbols (such as jewelry)
10. Paralanguage (speech rate, pitch, inflections, volume, pauses, and silence)
11. Color symbolism
12. Taste, including the symbolism of food and the communication function of chatting over coffee or tea
13. Cosmetics: temporary-powder, lipstick, or permanent, tattoos, plastic surgery
14. Time symbolism: What is too late or too early to telephone or visit a friend, or too long or too short to make a speech or stay for dinner.

Intercultural Negotiation

Managing Intercultural Negotiations

Closely related to managing political risks, but deserving special attention, is managing intercultural negotiations. Negotiation is the process of bargaining with one or more parties to arrive at a solution that is acceptable to all. Negotiation often come after political risk and can be used as an approach to conflict management. If the risk is worth it, then the MNC must negotiate with the host country to secure the best possible arrangements. The MNC and the host country will discuss the investment the MNC is prepared to make in return for certain guarantees and / or concessions. The initial range of topics typically will include critical areas such as hiring practices, direct financial investment, taxes, and ownership control. Negotiation also is used in creating joint ventures with local firms and in getting the operation off the ground. After the firm is operating, additional areas of negotiation often include expansion of facilities, use of more local managers, additional imports or exports of materials and finished goods, and recapture of profits.

On a macro level of international trends are the negotiations conducted between countries. The current balance-of-trade problems between the United States and china are one example. The massive debt problems of Third World countries and the opening of trade doors with Eastern European countries are other current examples.

The Negotiation process

There are several basic steps that can be used in managing the negotiation process. Regardless of the issues or personalities of the parties involved, this process typically begins with planning.

Planning

Planning starts with the negotiators' identifying those objectives they would like to attain. Then, they explore the possible options for reaching these objectives. Research shows that the greater the number of options, the greater the chances for successful negotiations. While this appears to be an obvious statement, research also reveals that many negotiators do not alter their strategy when negotiating across cultures. Consideration is usually given to areas of common ground between the parties. Other major areas include:
1. The setting of limits on single-point-objectives, such as deciding to pay no more than $10 million for the factory and $3 million for the land,
2. Dividing issues into short-end long-term considerations and deciding how to handle each; and
3. Determining the sequence in which to discuss the various issues.

Impersonal Relationship Building

The second phase of the negotiation process involves getting to know the people on the other side. This "feeling out" period is characterized by the desire to identify those who are reasonable and those who are not. In contrast to negotiations in many other countries, those in the United States often give little attention to this phase; they want to get down to business immediately, which often is an ineffective approach. Adler notes:

Effective negotiators must view luncheon, dinner, reception, ceremony, and the invitations as times for interpersonal relationship building, and therefore as key to the negotiating process. When American negotiators, often frustrated by the seemingly endless formalities, ceremonies, and "small talk", as how long they must wait before beginning to "do business", the answer is simple: wait until your opponents bring up business (and they will). Realize that the work of conducting a successful negotiation has already begun, even if business has yet to be mentioned.

Exchanging Task-Related Information

In this part of the negotiation process, each group sets forth its position on the critical issues. These positions often will change later in the negotiations. At this point, the participants are trying to find out what the other party wants to attain and what it is willing to give up.

Persuasion

This step of negotiation process is considered by many to be the most important. No side wants to give away more than it has to, but each knows that without giving some concessions, it is unlikely to reach a final agreement. The success of the persuasion step often depends on:
1. How well the parties understand each other's position
2. The ability of each to identify areas of similarity and differences;
3. The ability to create new options, and
4. The willingness to work toward a solution that allows all parties to walk away feeling they have achieved their objectives.

Agreement

The final phase of negotiations is the granting of concessions and detailing out a final agreement. Sometimes, this phase is carried out piecemeal, and concessions and agreements are made on issues one at a time. This is the way those from the United States like to negotiate. As each issue is resolved, it is removed from the bargaining table and interest focused on the next. Asians and Russians, on the other hand, tend to negotiate a final agreement on everything, and few concessions are given until the end. Simply put, to negotiate effectively in the international arena, it is necessary to understand how cultural differences between parties affect the process.

Cultural Differences Affecting Negotiations

In effective intercultural negotiation, it is important to have a sound understanding of the other side's culture. This includes consideration of areas such as communication patterns, time orientation, and social behaviors. A number of useful steps can help in this process. One negotiation expert recommends the following:-
1. Do not identify the counterpart's home culture too quickly. Common cues (e.g., name, physical appearance, language, accent, location) may be unreliable. The counterpart probably belongs to more than one culture.
2. Beware of the Western bias toward "doing". In Arab, Asian, and Latin groups, ways of being (e.g., compartment, smell), feeling, thinking, and talking can shape relationships more powerfully than doing.
3. Try to counteract the tendency to formulate simple, consistent, stable images.
4. Do not assume that all aspects of the culture are equally significant. In Japan, consulting all relevant parties to a decision is more important than presenting a gift.
5. Recognize that norms for interactions involving outsiders may differ from those for interactions between compatriots.
6. Do not overestimate your familiarity with your counterpart's culture. An American studying Japanese wrote New Year's wishes to Japanese contacts in basic Japanese characters, but omitted one character. As a result, the message became "Dead man, congratulations".

Other useful examples have been offered by Trompenaars and Hampden-Turner, who noted that a society's culture often plays a major role in determining the effectiveness of a negotiating approach. This is particularly true when the negotiating groups come from decidedly different cultures such as an ascription society and an achievement society. An ascription society status is attributed based on birth, kinship, gender, age and personal connections. In an achievement society status is determined by accomplishments. As a result, each side's cultural perceptions can affect the outcome of the negotiation. A good example:

Sending whiz-kids to deal with people 10-20 years their senior often insults the inscriptive culture. The reaction may be: "Do these people think that they have reached our own level of experience in half the time? That a 30-year-old American is good enough to negotiate with a 50-year-old Greek or Italian?" Achievement cultures must understand that some inscriptive cultures, the Japanese especially, spend much on training and in-house education to ensure that older people actually are wiser for the years they have spent in the corporation and for the sheer number of subordinates briefing them. It insults an inscriptive culture to do anything which prevents the self-fulfilling nature of its beliefs. Older people are held to be important so that they will be nourished and sustained by others' respect. A stranger is expected to facilitate this scheme, not challenge it.

U.S. negotiators have a style that often differs from that of negotiators in many other countries. Americans believe it is important to be factual and objective. In addition, they often make early concessions to show the other party that they are flexible and reasonable. Moreover, U.S. negotiators typically have authority to bind their party to an agreement, so if the right deal is struck, the matter can be resolved quickly. This is why deadlines are so important to Americans. They have come to do business, and they want to get things resolved immediately.

A comparative example would be the Arabs, who in contrast to Americans, with their logical approach, tend to use an emotional appeal in their negotiation style. They analyze things subjectively and treat deadlines as only general guidelines for wrapping up negotiations. They tend to open negotiations with an extreme initial position. However, the Arabs believe strongly in making concessions, do so throughout the bargaining process, and almost always reciprocate an opponent's concessions. They also seek to build a long-term relationship with their bargaining partners. For these reasons, Americans typically find it easier to negotiate with Arabs than with representatives from many other regions of the world.

Another unique comparative example is provided by the Chinese. In initial negotiation meetings, it is common for these negotiators to seek agreement on the general focus of the meetings. The creating of specific details is postponed for later gatherings. By achieving agreement on the general framework within which the negotiations will be conducted, the Chinese thus seek to limit and focus the discussions. Most Westerners misunderstand what is happening during these initial meetings and believe the dialogue consists mostly of rhetoric and general conversation. They are wrong and quite often are surprised later on when the Chinese negotiators use the agreement on the framework and principles as a basis for getting agreement on goals, and then insist that all discussions on concrete arrangements be in accord with these agreed upon goals. Simply put, what is viewed as general conversation by many Western negotiators is regarded by the Chinese as a formulation of the rules of the game which must be adhered to throughout the negotiations. So in negotiating with the Chinese, it is important to come prepared to ensure that one's own agenda, framework, and principles are accepted by both parties.

Before beginning any negotiations, negotiators usually review the negotiating style of the other parties. (Table 1-9 provides some insights regarding the general negotiating style of the Americans, Japanese, Arabs, and Mexicans). This review should help to ensure certain questions: What we can expect the other negotiating party to say and do? How are they likely to respond to certain offers? When should the most important issues be introduced? How quickly should concessions be made, and what type of reciprocity should be expected? These types of questions help effectively prepare the negotiators. International negotiating teams will work on formulating negotiation tactics.

Negotiation Tactics

A number of specific tactics are used in international negotiation. The following discussion examines some of the most common.

Location

Where should negotiations take place? If the negotiation is very important, to both organizations, most firms will suggest a neutral site. For example, U.S. firms negotiating with companies from the Far East will met in Hawaii, South American companies negotiating with European firms will tend to meet halfway, say in New York City. There are a number of benefits derive from using a neutral site. One is that each party has limited access to its head office for receiving a great deal of negotiating information and advice and thus gaining an advantage on the other. A second is that the cost of staying at the site often is quite high, so both sides have an incentive to conclude their negotiations as quickly as possible. (In the case, when one side enjoys the facilities and would like to stay as long as possible, the negotiations could be extended). A third is that most negotiators do not like to return home with nothing to show for their efforts made, so they are usually motivated to come to some type of agreement.

Time Limits

Time limits are an important negotiation tactic when one party is under a time constraint. This is particularly true when this party has agreed to meet at the home site of the other party. For example, U.S. negotiators who go to London to discuss a joint venture with a British firm often will have a scheduled return flight. Once their hosts find out how long these individuals intend to say, the British can plan their strategy accordingly. The 'real' negotiations are unlikely to begin until close to the time that the Americans are about to leave.

Time limits can be used tactically even if the negotiators meet at a neutral site. For example, most Americans like to be home with their families for Thanksgiving, Christmas, and the New Year holiday. Negotiations held right before these dates put Americans at a disadvantage, because the other party knows when the Americans will leave.

Buyer-Seller Relations

How should buyers and sellers act? As noted earlier, Americans believe in being objective and trading favors. When the negotiation are over, Americans walk away with what they have received from the other party, and they expect the other party to do the same. This may not be the way negotiators in many other countries think though.

The Japanese, for example, believe that the buyers should get most of what they want. However, they also believe that the seller should be taken care through reciprocal favors. The buyer must ensure that the seller has not been "picked clean". For example, when many Japanese firms first started doing business with large U.S. firms, they were unaware of U.S. negotiating tactics. As a result, the Japanese thought the Americans were taking advantage of them, whereas the Americans believed they were driving a good, hard bargain. The Brazilians are quite different from both the Americans and Japanese.

Researchers have found that Brazilian do better when they are more deceptive and self-interested and their opponents more open and honest than they are. Brazilians also tend to make fewer promises and commitments than their opponents, and they are much more prone to say no. However, Brazilians are more likely to make initial concessions. Overall, Brazilians are more like Americans than Japanese in that they try to maximize their advantage, but they are unlike Americans in that they do not feel obligated to be open and forthright in their approach.

Table 1-9

Negotiation Styles from a Cross-Cultural Perspective

Element	United States	Japanese	Arabians	Mexicans
1) Group Composition	Marketing oriented	Function oriented	Committee of Specialists	Friendship oriented
2) Number involved Space orientation	2-3 Confrontational; Competitive	4-7 Display Status harmonious Relationship	4-6	2-3 Close, friendly
3) Establishing Rapport	Short period; direct to task	longer period until harmony	long period until trusted	longer period discuss family
4) Exchange of Information	Documented; step step; multimedia	Extensive, concentrate On receiving Side	Less emphasis on technology more on relationship	Less emphasis on technology more on relationship
5) Persuasion Tools	Time pressure, loss of saving/ Making money	Maintain relationship references; Inter-group Connections	Go-between hospitality	Emphasis on families and on social concerns; goodwill Measured to Generations
6) Use of Language	Open, direct, sense of urgency	Indirect, appreciative cooperative	Flattery, emotional, religious	Respectful, gracious.
7) First offer	Fair ±5 to 10%	±10 to 20%	±20to50%	Fair
8) Second offer	Add to package; sweeten the deal	-5%	-10%	Add on incentive
9) Final offer Package	Total package	Makes no further concessions	-25%	Total

10) Decision-making Process	Top management team	Collective	Team makes recommen-dation	Senior manager & secretary
11) Decision-maker	Top management team	Middle line with team consensus	Senior manager	Senior manager
12) Risk taking	Calculated personal responsibility	Low group responsibility	Religion based	Personally responsible

Bargaining Behaviors

Closely related to the topic of negotiation tactics are the different types of bargaining behaviors, including both verbal and non-verbal behaviors. Verbal behaviors are an important part of the negotiating process, because they can improve the final outcome. Research show that the profits of the negotiators increase when they make high initial offers, ask a lot of questions, and do not make many verbal commitments until the end of the negotiating process. In summary, verbal behaviors are critical to the success of negotiations.

Use of Extreme Behaviors

Some group of negotiators begin by making extreme offers or requests, the Chinese and Arabs are examples. Another group of negotiators, however, begin with an initial position that is close to the one they are seeking, here the Americans and Swedes are examples.

With comparison of both positions, is one approach better or more effective than the other? Research shows that extreme positions tend to produce better results. Some of the reasons relate to the fact that an extreme bargaining position:
1)   Shows the other party that the bargainer will not be exploited;
2)   Extends the negotiation and gives the bargainer a better opportunity to gain information on the opponent;
3)   Allows more room for concessions;
4)   Modifies the opponent's beliefs about the bargainer's preferences;
5)   Shows the opponent that the bargainer is willing to play the game according to the usual norms; and
6)   Let the bargainer gain more than would probably be possible if a less extreme initial position had been taken.

Example of extreme position, the Olympic Committee felt that the Japanese should pay $10 million for the right to televise the games in the country, so when the Japanese offered $6 million for the rights, the Olympic committee countered with $90 million. Finally, both sides agreed on $18.5 million. Through the effective use of extreme position bargaining, Peter Ueberroth got the Japanese to pay over three times their original offer, an amount well in excess of the committee's budget.

Promises, Threats, And Other Behaviors

Another approach to bargaining is the use of promises, threats, rewards, self-disclosures, and other behaviors that are designed to influence the other party. These behaviors often are greatly influenced by the culture. Graham conducted research using Japanese, U.S. , and Brazilian business people and found that they employed a variety of different behaviors during a buyer-seller negotiation simulation. Table 1-10 shows the result.

The table shows that Americans and Japanese make greater use of promises than Brazilians. The Japanese also rely heavily on recommendations and commitment. The Brazilians use a discussion of rewards, commends, and self-disclosure more than Americans and Japanese. The Brazilians also say no a great deal more and make first offers that have higher-level profits than those of the others. Americans tend to operate between these two groups, although they do make less use of commands than either of their opponents and make first offers that have lower profits levels than their opponents.

Nonverbal Behaviors

Nonverbal behaviors are also very present during negotiation. These behaviors refer to what people do rather than what they say. Nonverbal behaviors sometimes are called the "silent language". Typical examples include silent periods, facial gazing, touching, and conversational overlaps. As seen in Table 1-11, the Japanese tend to use silent periods much more often than either Americans or Brazilians during negotiations. In fact, in this study, the latter did not use them at all. The Brazilians did, however make frequent use of other nonverbal behaviors. They employed facial gazing almost four times more often than the Japanese and almost twice as often as the Americans. Furthermore, although the latter two groups did not touch their opponents, the Brazilians made wide use of this nonverbal tactic. They also relied heavily on conversational overlaps, employing them more than twice as often as the Japanese and almost three times as often as Americans. Quite obviously, the Brazilians rely very heavily on nonverbal behaviors in their negotiating.

The crucial thing to remember is that in intercultural negotiations, people use a wide variety of tactics, and the other side must be prepared to counter or find a way of dealing with them. The response will depend on the situation. Managers from different cultures will give different answers. Table 1-12 presents some examples of the types of characteristics needed in effective negotiators. The extent to which International managers adopt these characteristics, their role as negotiators is positively correlated to success.

Summary

Intercultural Negotiation is the process of bargaining with one or more parties to arrive at a solution that is acceptable to all. This process involves five basic steps: planning, interpersonal relationship building, exchanging task-related information, persuasion, and agreement. The method in which the process is carried out often varies because of cultural differences.

There is a wide variety of tactics use in international negotiating. These include location, time limits, buyer-seller relations, verbal behaviors, and non-verbal behaviors.

Table 1-10

Cross-Cultural Differences in Verbal Behavior of Japanese, U.S, and Brazilian Negotiators

Behavior and Definitions	Number of times tactic was used in Bargaining Session		
	Japanese	U.S.	Brazilian
1) Promise : A statement in which the source indicated an intention to provide the target with a reinforcing consequence which source anticipates target will evaluate as pleasant, positive, or rewarding.	7	8	3
2) Threat : Same as promise, except that the reinforcing consequences are thought to be noxious, unpleasant, or punishing	4	4	2
3) Recommendation : A statement in which the source predicts that a pleasant environmental consequence will occur to the target. Its occurrence is not under the source's control.	7	4	5
4) Reward : A statement by the source that is thought to create pleasant consequences for the target.	1	2	2

Behavior	Japanese	U.S.	Brazilian
5) Positive Normative Appeal : A statement in which the source indicates that the target's past, present, or future behavior was or will be in conformity with social norms.	1	1	0
6) Commitment : A statement by the source to the effect that its future bids will not go below or above a certain level.	15	13	8
7) Self-disclosure : A statement in which the source reveals information about itself.	34	36	39
8) First Offer : The profit level associated with each participant's first offers.	61.5	57.3	75.2
9) Initial concession : The differences in profit between the first and second offer.	6.5	9.0	83.4

Table 1-11

Cross-Cultural Differences In Nonverbal Behavior Of Japanese, U.S., and Brazilian Negotiators

	Number of times tactic was used in Bargaining Session		
Behavior and Definition	Japanese	U.S.	Brazilian
Silent Period : The number of Conversational gaps of 10 seconds Or more per 30 minutes	5.5	3.5	0
Facial Gazing : The number of Minutes negotiators spend looking At their opponent's face per randoming Selected 10-minute period	1.3	3.3	5.2
Touching : Incidents of bargainer's Touching one another per half-hour (not including handshakes)	0	0	4.7
Conversational Overlaps : The number Of times (per 10 minutes) that both parties To the negotiation would talk at the same Time.	12.6	10.3	28.6

Table 1-12

Cultural Specific Characteristics Needed By International Managers For Effective Negotiations

Managers

United States	Japan	Taiwan (Chinese)	Brazil
1. Preparation and planning skill	1. Dedication to job	1. Persistence and Determination	1. Preparation and planning skill
2. Ability to think under pressure	2. Ability to perceive and exploit power	2. Ability to win respect and confidence	2. Ability to think under pressure
3. Judgement and intelligence	3. Ability to win respect and confidence	3. Preparation and planning skill	3. Judgement and intelligence
4. Verbal Expressivenes	4. Integrity	4. Product knowledge	4. Verbal Expressiveness
5. Product Knowledge	5. Listening Skill	5. Interesting	5. Product Knowledge
6. Ability to perceive and exploit power integrity	6. Broad perspective	6. Judgement and intelligence	6. Ability to perceive and exploit power integrity
	7. Verbal Expressiveness		7. Competitiveness

Chapter Four

Human Resource In The Global Context

Introduction

In view of the recent technology advancements in almost every field of research and industry and the capability of communications available and easy access to information, the world seemed to have shrink. Some critics now termed the world as a global village. The word Globalization had been generated to popularity even known in some third world countries. Many organizations view globalization as a new avenue to business crossing home turf. Many MNCs and even medium size firms had begin this exodus of finding new markets in host countries.

These organizations exists for a variety of purposes. Some produce goods for local or overseas consumption, others provide necessary services for profit or community benefit. In the process of pursuing their objectives, most if not all firms rely on the availability and effectiveness of several kinds of resources, which can be divided into finances, technology and people. Some firms emphasize their financial resources, others rely on the sophistication of their technology (telecommunication manufacturing, information technology), while the growing service sector in America industry depends mainly on the quality of its employees, its human resources.

Regardless of the particular resources emphasis in an industry, the human resources is almost always the key ingredient for organizational success. People design, operate and repair the technology, people control the financial resources, and people manage other people in all organizations. Compared with technological or financial resources, employees (the human resources) are the most unpredictable, and the largest ongoing cost factor in any organization. It is therefore crucial that they managed effectively and that their personal and work needs are satisfied, if organizational objectives are to be achieved.

The management of employees in American industry has undergone many changes in this millennium, and has been influenced by a variety of theories, ideologies and their employees. Organizational restructuring and delayering, had placed emphasis on efficiency, quality and productivity.

The roles and activities of strategic human resource managers in ensuring that such approaches are effective are therefore crucial. A distinction needs to be drawn at this stage, however, between two common terms used to describe these roles and activities, 'personal management' and 'strategic human resource management'.

Personnel Management And Human Resource Management

Early employee specialists were called personnel managers (or personnel administrators), and this term is still in use. Personnel management refers to a set of functions or activities (eg., recruitment, selection, training, salary administration, industrial relations) often performed effectively but with little relationship between the various activities, or with overall organizational objectives.

In recent management theories, the concept of human resource management (HRM) has sharply influenced professional practice. HRM assumes that all personnel activities are integrated with each other, and strategically with organizational objectives. As Peter Coppleston explains, 'the HR function within any enterprise must first of all serve the organization, an investment unit rather than a cost to the organization. This view is reinforced by other writers who emphasize that human resources should be viewed as 'human capital', 'human assets' or 'intellectual capital', and that HR managers should strive to utilize them as 'critical investments' in an organization's future : 'the role of HRM is not just to rigidly implement a preconceived business strategy but, in fact, to create an environment in which the appropriate strategy is likely to emerge'.

Different perspectives of HRM emphasize either the effective management of employees through greater accountability and control, the greater involvement of employees in decision-making processes, or both of these.

There are many challenges to the human resource management function of any organization, domestic or international. Given the greater complexity of managing international operations, the need to ensure high quality management is even more critical than in domestic operations.

A crucial component of implementing global strategy is international human resource management (IHRM). IHRM is increasingly being recognized as a major determinant of success or failure in international business. One survey of 400 executives in European firms concluded that a shortage of qualified international mangers was the single most important constraint on expansion abroad. About a third of the companies surveyed had experienced difficulties in finding managers with an international outlook. These firms usually do not realize, however, that by sending managers overseas and managing their effective repatriation and retention, they can develop a management cadre with a global perspective and a familiarity with the company's interests and operations in its foreign subsidiaries. Such an international management cadre does not appear overnight. Corporations operating overseas need to pay careful attention to this most critical resource, one that also provides control over other resources. Most U.S. multinationals, recent studies show, had neglected the importance of the human resource planing function in the selection, training, acculturation, and evaluation of managers assigned abroad.

At the first level of planning, decisions are required on the staffing policy suitable for a focus kind of business, is global strategy, and its geographic locations. Key issues involve the difficulty of control in geographically dispersed operations, the need for local decision making independent of the home office, and the suitability of managers from alternate sources.

The interdependence of strategy, structure, and staffing is particularly worth nothing. Ideally, the desired strategy of the firm should dictate the organizational structure and staffing modes considered most effective for implementing that strategy. In reality, however, there is usually considerable interdependence among these functions. Existing structural constraints often affect strategic decisions; similarly, staffing constraints or unique sets of competence in management come into play in organizational and sometimes strategic decisions. It is therefore important to achieve a system of fits among those variable that facilitates strategic implementation.

International Labor Relations

One of the major challenges facing MNCs is that of orienting their strategy to meet the varying demands of organized labor around the world. National differences in economic, political, and legal systems create a variety of labor relations systems, and the strategy that is effective in one country or region can be of little value in another country.

In managing labor relations, most MNCs use a combination of centralization and decentralization with some decisions being made at headquarters and others being handled by managers on-site. Researchers have found that U.S. MNCs tend to exercise more centralized control in contrast to European MNCs such as the British. A number of factors have been cited to explain this development, including :-

1.   U.S. companies tend to rely heavily on formal management controls and a close reporting system is needed to support this process.
2.   European companies tend to deal with labor unions at an industry level compared to U.S. MNCs that deal at the company level, and
3.   For many U.S. firms the domestic market represents the bulk of their sales (a situation that is not true for many European MNCs) and the overseas market is managed as an extension of domestic operations.

Labor Relations Practices

Labor relations practices vary widely. In some countries the economy is strong and unions are able to make major demands; in other countries the economy is weak and the union's ability to bargain is diminished. In the same token, some countries have strong promanagement governments while others are heavily union-oriented. A third factor is the willingness of unions to strike or walk out as opposed to continuing to talk with management in the hopes of resolving differences. Germany and Japan have some interesting contrasts.

Germany

Labor unions have been traditionally strong in Germany. Although a minority of the labor force is organized, unions set the pay scale for about 90 percent of the country's workers with wages determined by job classifications. Union membership is voluntary, but there is only one union in each major industry. This union will negotiate a contract with the employers' federation for the industry, and the contrast will cover all major issues, including wages and terms of employment. If there is a disagreement over the interpretation or enforcement of the contract, the impasse is typically resolved between the company and the worker with the participation of a union representation or work council. If this procedure is unsuccessful, the matter can then be referred to a German labor court for final settlement.

Despite their power, unions have a much more cooperative relationship with management than do their counterparts in the United States. One reason is that workers serve on the board of directors and can endure that the rank-and-file are treated fairly.

If there is a strike, it tends to occur after the contract has run out and a new one has yet to be ratified by the workers. As in the United States, several may be in force in a particular firm, and these agreements do not have the same termination dates. Usually our group of workers may be striking or working without a contract while another is working under contract. Instances and in violation of law, there may be strikes in the middle of a contract period, but this is exceptional and in many cases the union and management typically have a good working relationship.

Japan

In Japan, union-management relationships are extremely cooperative. Social custom dictates non-confrontational behavior. So although labor agreements are often general and vague, disputes regarding interpretations tend to be settled in an amicable manner. Sometimes it is necessary to bring in third-party mediators or arbitrators, but there are no prolonged, acrimonious disputes that end up in a plant being closed down because the two sides cannot work together.

Typically, a strike is used merely to embarrass the management and seldom lasts longer than one week. While it is possible to resort to legal action in resolving strikes, this is typically frowned upon by both labor and management and both sides try to stay away from using this means of bringing about solutions to their problems.

Japanese unions are most active during the spring and at the end of the year, the two periods during which bonuses are negotiated. However, these activities do not usually end up in a union, management conflict. If there is a strike, it is more likely when a Japanese union is negotiating with management during industry wide negotiations. Even here, the objective is to show that the workers are supportive of the union and not to indicate a grievance or complaint with management. In overall terms, Japanese workers tend to subordinate their interests and identifies to those of the group. This cultural value helps to account for a great deal of the harmony that exists between unions and management.

Industrial Democracy

Different from the United States, many countries have industrial democracy, which is the legally mandated right of employees to participate in significant management decisions. This authority extends into areas such as wages, bonuses, profit sharing, work rules, dismissals, and plant expansions and closings. Industrial democracy can take a number of different forms.

Forms of Industrial Democracy

At present there are a number of forms of industrial democracy. In some countries one form may be more prevalent than others, and it is common to find some of these forms existing simultaneously. The following are three most popular forms:-

Co-determination

Co-determination is a legal system that requires workers and their managers to discuss major strategic decision before firms implement them. Codetermination has brought about workers participation on boards of directors and is quite popular in Europe, where in Austria, Denmark, Holland and Sweden there is legally mandated codetermination. In many cases the workers hold one-third of the seats on the board, although it is 50 percent in private German firms with 2,000 or more employees. On the negative side, some researchers report that many workers are unimpressed with codetermination and feel that it does not provide sufficient workers input to major decisions.

Work Councils

Work Councils are groups that consist of both worker and manager representatives and are charged with dealing with matters such as improving firm performance, working conditions, and job security. In some firms these councils are worker or union, run, whereas in other companies a management representative chairs the group. These councils are a result of either national legislation or collective bargaining at the company-union level, and they exist throughout Europe. However, the power of these councils varies. In Germany, the Netherlands, and Italy, work councils are more powerful than they are in England, France, and Scandinavia.

Shop Floor Participation

Shop floor participation takes many forms, including job enrichment programs, quality circles, and various other versions of participative management. These approaches provide the workers with an opportunity to make their voices heard and to play a role in identifying problems and resolving them. Shop floor participation is widely used in Scandinavian countries and has spread to other European nations and to the United States over the last decade.

Action in Industrial Democracy

Industrial democracy can be found in different forms throughout the United States, Europe and Asia. The following examines three examples:-

Germany

Industrial democracy and codetermination are both very strong in Germany, especially in the steel and auto industries. Private firms with 2,000 or more employees (in the steel industry it is 1,000 employees) must have supervisory boards (similar to a board of directors in the United States) composed of workers as well as managers. There must also be a management board which is responsible for daily operations, and company employees elect members to this board.

Researchers have found that co determinism works well in Germany. Some critics have argued that there are too many people involved in the decision-making process, and this slows things down, thus resulting in inefficiencies. However, Scholl reports that a study he conducted of both of manager and work councils found no such problems. In fact, the 1990s are likely to see even greater efforts toward co determinism in a unified Germany.

Denmark

Industrial democracy in Denmark gives workers the right to participate in management on both a direct and an indirect basis. The direct form maintains that employees are members of semiautonomous work groups that provide ideas on how to enhance productivity and quality and schedule work. In indirect form there are shop stewards on the flow who represent the workers, fellow workers on the board of directors, and co-operation committees that consist of both management and worker representatives. Industrial democracy works exceptionally well in Denmark, where researchers have found that co-operation committees contribute substantially to openness, co-ordination of effort, and a feeling of importance on the part of workers.

Japan

Japan's use of industrial democracy concepts is not tied to political philosophy as is the case in Europe; rather it is oriented more of Japanese culture and the belief in group harmony. Moreover, Japanese industrial democracy is not as extensive as that in the west. Japanese workers are encouraged to identify and help to solve job-related problems associated with quality and the flow of work management in turn is particularly receptive to worker ideas that will produce bottom-line results. This process is carried out in a paternalistic setting in which the company looks after the employees and the latter respond appropriately.

Unions play virtually no role in promoting industrial democracy or participative management because they are weak and in many cases, only ceremonial. One group of researchers put it this way.

In truth, most workers think of themselves as company employees who are simply associated with the union. Moreover, it is not uncommon to find a union strike in a company with two or three work shifts and no loss of work output. This is because when the strikers are done picketing or marching, they then go to work and the group coming out of the factory takes up the strike activity. In a factory with three shifts, a line employee will work a full shift, picket for a while, go home to eat and sleep, and then return to the factory for her or his shift.

As a result, Japanese MNCs face the greatest challenge from industrial democracy during the 1990s because they one least accustomed to using the idea. On the other hand, as Japanese firms continue to expand into Europe and the United States, it is likely that there will be a growing use of authority-sharing concepts such as codetermination, work councils and other approaches that are becoming so common in western firms.

Human Resources : Managing Foreign Expatriates

Managing Employee Performance Overseas

The ultimate evaluation of the performance of expatriates and their workforce rests with the business results and outcomes achieved at the completion of the overseas assignment. Was the overseas operation effectively established (or has it grown)? Were new product markets successfully developed, and was the return on investment the best that could have been achieved during the period? Was the necessary network (eg. Customers, suppliers, governments) for future organizational growth established?

The answers to these broad business questions will necessarily depend on such factors as:-

1. The reality (or unreality) of business strategies.
2. The nature of the overseas venture (eg. Joint venture, strategic alliance, multinational and the level of support given by the parent company, the stability (eg. Social, political, economic) of the host country environment.
3. The relevance of staffing strategies (eg. Mix of home, host and third country nationals, skills and competency levels, etc)

The standards of business performance (or benchmarks) against which such performance indicators are measured (e.g. Regional countries, global standards, home country levels) also need to be factored into the determination of the effectiveness of the expatriate's performance Are they too high, too low, or just right?

An example, an expatriate manager may be assessed as a very effective performer because they met (or exceeded) sales targets, even though they alienated their local subordinates or damaged good relationships with host country governments through overaggressive methods. Conversely, an expatriate manager may be regarded as an under-achiever if they fail to meet financial goals because of problems with suppliers, local industrial relations difficulties or a focus on longer-term governmental relationships.

These examples suggest that the assessment of an expatriate's performance needs to take into account not only the outcomes they achieve, but also the environmental issues they face in diverse host countries, and the short and long-term benefits of their activities. For least and third country nationals, performance appraisal and management schemes may need to be different from those familiar to the parent firms, in order to appropriately reflect the different socio-cultural environments in which they operate.

Expatriate performance Criteria and Competencies

Mendenhall and Oddon suggest that the broad international skills that expatriates must exhibit during their overseas assignment include:-

1.   being able to manage a workforce with cultural and sub-cultural differences
2.   being able to plan for, and conceptualize, the dynamics of a complex multi-national environment
3.   being open-minded about alternative methods for solving problems
4.   being flexible in dealing with people and systems, and
5.   understanding the interdependencies among the firm's domestic and foreign operations.

These broad expatriate performance criteria encapsulate the need for cross-cultural management competencies, and postulate that the identified achievements of expatriate managers are directly transferable to the management of operations back in the home country, Firms, therefore, neglect or fail to appreciate the value of such competencies to have country operations do so at their own risk.

More significantly, Mendenhall and Oddon suggest that the relevant performance criteria for expatriates should include (at least) their 'technical information and expertise', 'adjustment to the new culture' and 'environmental factors' Dowing agrees with the need to factor ' environment' issues (eg. Industrial relations, social and economic factors) into performance evaluation schemes, but adds that 'task' (ie. The nature of the expatriate's job, the length of the assignment, the degree of required interaction with the host country) and 'personality' issues (ie. Qualities of the expatriate and their families relevant to the host country) may be equally as important. Both emphasize that the appraisal of expatriates may need to differ from methods used in the home country, in order to properly take into account the diverse characteristics of the foreign environment.

Thus, the evaluation of expatriate performance may use different criteria or different levels of effectiveness in different countries of operation. An American firm operating in Hong Kong, Indonesia, Singapore and India (for example) will need to set variable performance standards and to measure them sensitively in relation to developments in the diverse host countries.

Performance appraisal schemes for such expatriates will both:

a)   need to modify criteria to fit the overseas position and country characteristics, and
b)   include an expatriate's insights as part of the evaluation.

The latter aspect acknowledges that the performance appraisal of expatriates is ideally a joint process involving host country mangers (and / or peers and subordinates), parent firm senior managers and the expatriates themselves.

Whilst all of these assessments may be inherently bias (for example, host country employees will perceive performance from their own cultural frames of reference, parent firm managers will usually suffer from the 'tyranny' of distance; expatriates are likely to be highly subjective), the combination of views included is likely to be more accurate than the appraisal completed by single parent firm manager. In some countries, local employees may be reluctant to express their negative perceptions of expatriates due to 'hierarchical' or 'face' issues.

Appraisal of the expatriate is, however, an important function for the business itself and for the expatriate. For the business, it indicates some of the potential (or actual) problems likely to be faced in pursuit of its objectives and may suggest practical solutions or more appropriate criteria for subsequent expatriates. For the expatriates themselves, performance appraisals may influence their promotion potential and type of position received on returning to their home country.

The Expatriate System – A Process Model

Expatriates are important members of an international system of management. They are the field operatives that link global activities to parent company interests, and they are often the vanguard, the adventurers, that break new ground for their firms. A company anticipates that expatriates provide an element of home country control over foreign operations; they act as insiders in distant facilities, dealing with the externalities of international markets and foreign workforce. Expatriates view themselves as set apart from the normal system of management. They step out of their parent-company hierarchies, risking alienation from domestic activities. The expatriate system is distinct from a company's domestic system creating a particular career cycle as a process during which an employee experience various stages of career changes, success for both the company and the employee depend on careful management of these developments.

This career cycle is a useful model for international human resource management because it emphasizes a sequence of activities that all companies must address when staffing foreign posts with expatriates. The cycle beings with recruitment and selection, a sensitive responsibility because few employees bring foreign work experience to their assignments or understand what they may entail. Hence, recruiters have difficulties evaluating how candidates will perform in the field. Further, candidates who may be interested in a foreign assignment may have family responsibilities that would present problems. For example, spouses' careers may be disrupted, and children may be uprooted from heir schools and friend.

The second part of the cycle is concerned with preparing employees for assignments. This activity involves pre-departure training and preparation for new cultural experiences. Once expatriates arrive at their foreign posts, they face new challenges of working and living abroad. During this phase, they experience significant changes in their lives and a different period of adaptation.

Assuming that they succeed in their assignments and return home, they must then readapt to their home environments. This final stage of repriatriation can bring difficulties of its own, because expatriates cannot simply arrive home and resume old jobs. Their old jobs are probably filled, but few want their old jobs back. They prefer new challenges, because they return with stronger career profiles and international experience that they want to apply. Some do resume their old jobs, and others are promoted into positions that make good use of their international experience, but many expatriates find themselves isolated in demeaning jobs. Those who feel disenfranchised often move on to different companies looking for opportunities to leverage their international acumen. Firms need effective repatriation programs to help home-board expatriates re-established themselves. The expatriates' family members also must readjust to home environments, and those who have been away for many years may encounter difficulties. Consequently, this cycle of activities represents a system of exciting but perplexing changes. Success or failure depends on how well a company supports its expatriates and on how well expatriates adapt to the circumstances they experience. The American society of personnel Administration International (ASPAI) has suggest that international firms should implement comprehensive programs composed of 3 components : Preparation, Adaptation, and Repatriation.

Preparation

In broad terms, the preparation stage includes recruitment, selection, orientation, and training activities. Recruitment resembles internal searches to evaluate potential candidates determine their qualifications, and develop a short list of those who seen best suited for a foreign assignment. Selection activities start with interview with candidates, and in the best programs it also includes interviewing family members who would accompany the employee overseas. Selection also includes skills testing (such as validation of language capability), psychological evaluations (such as assessment of the candidate's motivation and adaptability), and professional evaluations (such as assessments of individual characteristics such as leadership skills).

Orientation activities prepare the expatriate for entering a foreign society. Relatively simple activities include obtaining entry vision and inoculations. This step also involves complicated activities such as preparing for the culture shock of living in a foreign country. Orientation implies a form of briefing, while training implies a systematic effort to prepare the expatriate for both technical and social requirements of the foreign assignment. Therefore, pre-departure training can range from rather simple activities to thorough and extensive instruction; the choice depends on the nature of the assignment and the capabilities of the candidate. For example, a firm may send managers bound for Russia to intensive language courses, programs of study about the country's daily life and social customs, and instruction sessions in practical problems such as negotiation tactics. In contrast, a U.S. manager assigned to the United Kingdom will need no formal language instruction, but the societies are sufficiently different to warrant some cultural sensitivity training.

Adaptation

Activities associated with adaptation begin prior to leaving home, often as part of a formal training process. These preliminary training sessions are designed to ease the impact of moving to a new society by addressing topics such as acculturation, foreign currencies, housing, social customs, education, medical services, and foreign laws. Some organizations invite family members to participate in training programs, but the practice is not yet commonly known. During the adaptation stage, IHRM focuses on efforts to successfully position the expatriate in the foreign post and then to provide on going support during the often difficult time of adjustment to the new environment. This long-term effort begins with pre-departure planning, and it extends throughout the assignment period until the expatriate prepares to return home.

Repatriation

Near the end of a foreign assignment, an expatriate begins to focus attention on returning home. Some accept transfers to other foreign assignments, and they focus on those transitions. In either case, repatriation begins before the expatriate actually leaves the existing assignment. Initial IHRM activities are concerned with preparing the expatriate for re-entry, including arrangements for the physical logistics of relocation, travel, paying local income taxes, and "clearing the country". Expatriates often express interest in their next assignments or home jobs, and IHRM staff must provide a conduit of information related to job responsibilities and new role expectations. Expatriates returning home with families encounter additional considerations with transportation, housing, and dependent schooling. IHRM activities are therefore concerned with minimizing the pain associated with readjustment. In addition, expatriates who return from long or difficult foreign assignments may face substantial psychological adjustment problems.

Figure 1-21

Expatriate International Career Cycle

Return

Home-country

Assignment

Re-entry   Recruitment

Selection

Debriefing   Orientation

Foreign-country
Assignment

Figure 1-22

Components and Activities for a Comprehensive Expatriate Program

Preparation   Adaptation   Repatriation
Pre-departure Activities   Host-country Activities   Re-entry Activities

Job Criteria Planning	Arrival Sponsorship	Pre-return Orientation
Recruitment	Family Settlement	Home Leave Adjustment
Assessment/Selection	Housing and Supplies	Compensation Review
Orientation	Visa/Resident Permits	Career Review and Job
Employee Training	Tax Registration	Orientation
Contract Classification	Car or Transportation	Family Orientation
Career Planning	Job Orientation	Accommodation
Family Counseling	Compensation and	Resettlement Support
Orientation/Training	Benefits Management	Acculturation Training
Relocation Details	Parent/Host Linkage	Debriefing

Human Resources : Staffing, Training and Organizational Development Staffing For International Firms

Appropriate philosophies of managerial staffing abroad are known as the ethnocentric, polycentric, regiocentric, and geocentric approaches. Firms using an ethnocentric staffing approach fill key managerial positions with people from headquarters, that is, parent country nationals (PCNs). There are advantages of this approach, as PCNs are familiar with the organization goals, policies, and procedures, they know how to get things accomplished through headquarters. This policy is likely to be used where a company notice the inadequacy of local managerial skills and determines an essential need to maintain close communication and co-ordination with headquarters. It is also a preference choice when the organization has been organized around a centralized approach to globalization.

Very often, firms use PCNs for the top management positions in the foreign subsidiary, in particular, the Chief Executive Officer (CEO) and the Chief Financial Officer (CFO) to maintain close control. PCNs are usually preferable where a high level of technical capability is required. They are usually chosen for new international venture requiring managerial experience in the parent company and where there is a concern for loyalty to the firm rather than to the host country, in cases, for example, where proprietary technology is used extensively.

The disadvantages of the ethnocentric approach include:-

1)   Lack of opportunities or development for local managers, thereby decreasing their moral and their loyalty to the subsidiary, and

2)   The poor adaptation and lack of effectiveness of expatriates in foreign countries. Procter & Gamble, for example, routinely appointed managers from its headquarters for foreign assignments for many years. After several bad experiences in Japan, the firm realized that such a practice was insensitive to local cultures and also underutilized its pool of high potential non-American managers. In addition, an ethnocentric recruiting approach does not enable the company to take advantage of its worldwide pool of management skill.

This approach also serves to perpetuate certain personnel selections and other decision-making processes because the same types of people are making the same types of decisions.

With a polycentric staffing approach, local managers, host-country managers (HCNs) are hired to fill key positions in their own country. This approach is more likely to be effective when implementing a global strategy of regionalization. If a firm wants to "act local", there are obvious advantages to staffing with HCNs. These managers are naturally familiar with local culture, language, and ways of doing business, and they already have many contracts in place. HCNs are more likely to be accepted by people both inside and outside the subsidiary, and they provide role models for other upwardly mobile personnel. From the cost aspect, it is usually less expensive for a firm to hire a local manager than to transfer one from headquarters, frequently with a family and often at a higher rate of pay. Transferring personnel from headquarters is a particularly expensive policy when it turns out that the manager and her or his family do not adjust and have to be transferred home prematurely. In fact, rather than building their own facilities, some companies acquire foreign firms as a means of obtaining qualified local personnel. The upside potential in local managers is that they tend to be instrumental in starving off or more effectively dealing with problems in sensitive political situations. In some countries, in fact, have legal requirements that a specific proportion of the firm's top managers must be citizens of that country.

One disadvantage of a polycentric staffing policy is the difficulty of co-ordinating activities and goals between the subsidiary and the parent firm, including the potentially conflicting loyalties of the local manger. Poor co-ordination among subsidiaries of a multinational firm could constrain strategic options. A further drawback of this policy is that the headquarters managers of multinational firms will not gain the overseas experience necessary for any higher positions in the firm that require the understanding co-ordination of subsidiary operations.

In the geocentric staffing approach, the best managers are recruited within or outside of the company, regardless of nationality, a practice used for some time by many European multinationals. In the last decade, as more major U.S. firms began to globalize, they also consider hiring foreign executives for their top positions (for example, about 7 to 10% of high-level assignments in U.S. Many MNCs went for foreign managers in the last decade, compared to only 1% in 1986. In 1992, General Motors hired J. Ignacio Lopex de Arriortua as vice president for worldwide purchasing, Xerox hired Vittorio Casoni as executive vice-president, and Esprit de Corp hired Fritz Ammann as president. There are various important advantages of placing third-country nationals (TCNs) in subsidiaries. First, this policy provides a greater pool of qualified and willing applicants from which to choose, which in time, results in further development of an international executive cadre. Second, third-country nationals often bring more cultural flexibility and adaptability to a situation than parent-country nationals, especially if they are from a similar cultural background as the host-country co-workers and are accustomed to moving around. In addition, the placement of TCNs in key positions is perceived by employees as an acceptable compromise between headquarters and local managers and this helps to reduce resentment. Third, it can be more cost-effective to transfer and pay managers from some countries than from others because their pay scale and benefits packages are lower.

In a regiocentric staffing approach, recruiting is done on a regional basis, say within Latin America for a position in Chile. This staffing approach can produce a specific mix of PCNs, HCNs, and TCNs, according to the needs of the company or the product strategy.

What are the factors that influence the choice of staffing policy? Among them are the strategy and organizational structure of the firm as well as the factors related to the particular subsidiary (such as the duration of the particular foreign operation, the types of technology used, and the production and marketing techniques necessary). Factors related to the host country also play a part. (For example, the level of economic and technological development, political stability, regulations regarding ownership and staffing, and the sociocultural setting). From a practical perspective, however, the choice often depends on the availability of qualified managers in the host country. A large number of MNCs use a greater proportion of PCNs (also called expatriates) in top management positions, staffing middle and lower management positions with increasing proportion of HCNs as one moves down the organizational hierarchy.

The choice of staffing policy has a considerable influence on organizational variables in the subsidiary, such as the locus of decision-making authority, the methods of communication, and the perpetuation of human resource management practices. The ranges of variables are illustrated in Exhibit 1-4. The ethnocentric staffing approach, for example, usually results in a higher level of authority and decision making in headquarters compared to the polycentric approach.

Without prejudice or reservations, all phases of human resources management should be in support of the desired strategy of the firm. In the staffing function, having the right people in the right places at the right times is a key ingredient to success in international operations. An effective managerial cadre can be a distinct competitive advantage for an organizational. From surveys made in the past by 144 American, Western European, and Japanese firms, for their foreign subsidiaries. It is noted that the American and European firms used host-country nationals more in developed than in less developed countries for all management levels,. However, Japanese firms use more parent-country nationals at upper levels of management and did not use third-country nationals at all.

Exhibit 1-4

Organizational Effects of Staffing Orientation

ORIENTATION

Aspects of the firm	Ethnocentric	Polycentric	Regiocentric	Geocentric
1. Complexity of organization	Complex in home country, simple in subsidiaries	Varied and independent	Highly interdependent on a regional basis	Increasingly complex and highly inter-dependent on a world-wide basis
2. Authority, decision making	High in headquarters	Relatively low in headquarters	High regional headquarters and / or high collaboration among subsi-diaries	Collaboration of headquarter and subsi-diaries around the world
3. Evaluation and control	Home standards applied for persons and performance	Determined locally	Determined regionally	Standards which are universal and local

	Ethnocentric	Polycentric	Regiocentric	Geocentric
4. Rewards and punishments incentives	High in head quarters, low in subsidiaries	Wide variations can be high or low rewards for subsidiary performance	Rewards for contribution to regional objectives	Rewards to international and local executives for reaching local and worldwide objectives
5, Communication, information flow	High volume of orders, commands, advice to subsidiaries	Little to and from head-quarters; little among subsidiaries.	Little to and from corporate headquarters, but may be high to and from regional HQ and among countries	Both ways and among subsidiaries around the world
6. Geographical identification	Nationality of owner	Nationality of host country	Regional company	Truly world-wide company but identifying with national interests.
7. Perpetuation (recruiting, staffing, development)	People of home country developed for key positions everywhere in the world	People of local nationality developed for key positions in their own country	Regional people developed for key positions anywhere in the region	Best people everywhere in the world developed for key positions everywhere in the world

Selection

The selection of personnel for overseas assignments is a complex process. The criteria for selection are based on the same success factors as in the domestic setting, but additional criteria must be considered, related to the specific circumstances of each international position. More often than not, many personnel directors have a long-standing; internalize practice of selecting potential expatriates simply on the basis of their domestic track record and their technical expertise. Usually overlooked is the need to ascertain whether potential expatriates have the necessary cross-cultural awareness and interpersonal skills for the position. Another important aspect is to assess whether the candidate's personal and family situation is such that everyone is likely to adapt to the local culture. Ronan recently concluded that there are five categories of success for expatriate managers: job factors, relational dimensions, motivational state, family situation, and language skills, as shown in Exhibit 1-5. The relative importance of each factor is highly situational and difficult to establish.

These expatriate success factors are based on studies of American expatriates. One could argue that the requisite skills are the same for managers from any country and particularly so for third-country nationals.

A more flexible approach to maximizing managerial talent, regardless of the source, would certainly consider more closely whether the position could be suitably filled by a host-country national, as reflected in a model by Tang, based on her research. This contingency model of selection and training depends on the variables of the particular assignment, such as the period of stay, the similarity with the candidate's own culture, and the level of interaction with local managers in that job. Tung concludes that the more rigorous the selection and training process, the lower the failure rate.

The selection process is illustrated in Exhibit 1-6. It is frame-up as a decision tree in which the progression to the next stage of selection or the type of orientation training depends on the assessment of critical factors regarding the job or the candidate at each decision point. The simplest selection process involves choosing a local national, minimal training is necessary. The longest and most complex path to complete the selection and preparation process is created when all of the following conditions exist: the position cannot be filled by a local national: the job require a high level of interaction with the local community, the candidate wants the job; the target culture is very different from that of the candidate, and the candidate's relational abilities and family situation are important factors.

Most if not all MNCs used to start out their operations in a particular region by selecting primarily from their own pool of managers. Over time, and with increasing internationalization, they tend to move to a predominantly polycentric or regiocentric policy because of:-

1. increasing pressure (explicit or implicit) from lcoal governments to hire locals (or sometimes legal restraints on the use of expatriates), and
2. the greater costs of expatriate staffing, particularly when the firm has to pay taxes for the parent-company employee in both countries. In addition, in recent years, MNCs have noted an improvement in the level of managerial and technical competence in many countries, negating the main reason for using a primarily ethnocentric policy in the past. One researcher's comment represents a growing attitude: "All things being equal, a local national who speaks the language, understands the culture and the political system, and is often a member of the local elite, should be more effective than an expatriate aliens. The concerns about the need to maintain strategic control over subsidiaries and to develop managers with an international perspective remain a source of debate about staffing policies among human resource management professionals.

For MNCs based in Europe and Asia, human resource policies at all levels of the organization are greatly influenced by the home-country culture and policies. For Japanese subsidiaries in Singapore, Malaysia, and India, for example, promotion from within and expectations of long term loyalty to and by the firm are culture based transferable to subsidiaries. At Matsushita, the selection criteria for staffing seem to be similar to those of Western firms. The candidates are selected on the basis of a set of characteristics the firm calls SMILE: Specialty (required skill, knowledge); Management ability (particular motivational ability): international flexibility (adaptability): language facility; and endeavor (perseverance in the face of difficulty).

The decision on a staffing policy and selecting suitable managers are reasonable steps but do not itself ensure success. Many other reasons, besides poor selection, contributed to expatriate failure among U.S. multinationals. Many of these failures are the result of poor preparation an planning for the entry and reentry transitions of the manager and his or her family One very important variable consideration, for example, often neglected in the selection, preparation and support phases, is the suitability and adjustment of the spouse. The inability of the spouse to adjust to the new environment has been failure in U.S. and European firms. Yet only about half of those firms studied did include the spouse in the interviewing process. Furthermore although research shows that human relational skills are critical for overseas work (a fact acknowledged by the firms in a study by Tung), most of the U.S. firms surveyed failed to include this factor in their assessment of candidates.

A synthesis of the factors frequently mentioned by researchers and firms as the major causes of expatriate failure is as listed:-

1.   selection based on headquarters criteria rather than assignment needs.
2.   Inadequate preparation, training, and orientation prior to assignment
3.   Alienation or lack of support from headquarters
4.   Inability to adapt to local culture and working environment
5.   Problems with spouse and children, poor adaptation, family unhappiness
6.   Insufficient compensation and financial support
7.   Poor programs for career support and repatriation

After careful selection based on specific assignment and long-term plans both of the firm and the candidates, plans for preparation, training and development of expatriate managers are made.

Exhibit 1-5

Success Factors For International Expatriates

Job factors

Technical skills

Acquaintance with host-country and headquarters operations

Managerial skills

Administrative competence

Relational Dimensions

Tolerance for ambiguity

Behavioral flexibility

Nonjudgementalism

Cultural empathy and low ethnocentism

Interpersonal skills

Motivational state

Belief in the Mission

Congruence with career path

Interest in overseas experience

Interest in the specific host-country culture

Willlingness to acquire new patterns of behavior and attitudes

Family situation

Willingness of spouse to live abroad

Adaptive and supportive spouse

Stable marriage

Language skills

Host-country language

Nonverbal communication

Exhibit 1-6

The Selection Process

Start The Selection Process
Can the position be filled   Yes
by a local national

Select local national and subject him
or her to training basically aimed at
improving technical and managerial
skills

No

Identify degree of interaction
required with local community
using a 7 or 9 point scale, ranging   Low
from low to high, indicate the degree
of interaction with local community
required for successful performance
on the job

Emphasis on task variables. Second
(but by no means unimportant)
High   question is to ask whether the
individual is willing to serve abroad

Is candidate willing ?

No   Yes

No

Probably not   Start
suitable for   orientation
Probably not suitable
for position   position   (moderate to
                                                        low rigor)

Yes

Very Similar   Identify degree of similarity.
                                              Dissimilarity between cultures
Emphasis on task variables   using a 7 or 9 point scale, ranging
                                              from similar to highly diverse, indicate
                                              the magnitude of differences between
                                              the two cultures

Start orientation (moderate   Highly diverse
to high rigor)
                                              Emphasis on "relationalabilities factor"
                                              "Family situation factor" must also be
                                              taken into consideration

                                              Start orientation
                                              (most rigorous)

Training And Development

It is obvious that preparation and training for cross-cultural interactions is crucial. The need for expatriate managers to be culturally sensitive to the particular country is important. A survey conducted by some researchers indicated that up to 40% of expatriate managers and their foreign assignments early because of poor performance or an inability to adjust to the local environment. About half of those who do remain, function at a low level of effectiveness. An estimate was done on the cost of failed expatriate assignment. The direct cost itself is estimated to be ranging from $50,000 to $150,000. The indirect costs may be far greater, depending on the position held by the expatriate. Relations with the host-country government and customers may be damaged, resulting in a lost of market share and a poor reception for future PCNs.

Cross-cultural training has proved to be effective in many MNCs, but remorsefully from surveys conducted, only a third of expatriates are given such training. Much of the rationale for not sending the expatriate for cross-cultural training, is base on an assumption that managerial skills and processes are universal and therefore overlooked. In a simplistic way, a manager's domestic track record is used as the deciding selection criterion for an overseas assignment. The malpractice of equating domestic performance against International assignment is a very bias rationale though. Although there are merits in this assumption that managers that does well domestically, will likely also to do well in the international arena. Although this assumption is completely abstract and cannot to a certain extent be rejected fully. But dimensions like cultural backgrounds, communications through languages, the way of life and philosophies an perspectives of the host country should not be neglect and totally ignored. These are some of the knowledge and traits that even home country top performing mangers had to know and be trained in. Having noted the cost of failure, given the surveyed estimates on cost, therefore it is imperative for any organization not to overlook this area of training, preparation, and development of the selected local managers to be assigned overseas.

In most overseas assignments, however, the success of the expatriate is not left so much to chance. Many foreign firms provide considerably more training and preparation for expatriates than American firms. Unlike the Japanese multinationals, their recall rates stood below 5 percent, signifying that they send abroad managers who are far better prepared and more adapt at working and flourishing in a foreign environment. Success is largely attributable to training programs, it is also a result of intelligent planning by the human resource management staff in most Japanese firms, as reported in a study by Tung. This planning begins with a careful selection process for overseas assignments, based on the long-term knowledge of executives and their families. An effective selection process, of course, does eliminate many potential "failures" from the start.

The demands on expatriate managers are so much a result of the multiple relationships that they have to maintain as they are from different cultural background in the host-country environment. Exhibit 1-7 depicts those relations; note the inclusion of family relations. It is crucial to identify any potential problems that an expatriate may experience with those relationships so that these problems may be addressed during pre-departure training. Problem identification and recognition in the first stage in the comprehensive plan by Rahim for developing expatriates shown in Exhibit 1-8. According to Mendenhall and Oddon, the three areas critical to preparation are cultural training, language instruction, and familiarity with everyday matters. In the model shown in Exhibit 1-8, various development methods are used to address these areas during pre-departure training, post arrival training, and re-entry training. A two-way feedback between the executive and the trainers at each stage helps to tailor the level and kinds of training to the individual manager. The desired goal is the increased effectiveness of the expatriate as a result of familiarity with local conditions, cultural awareness, and an appreciation of his or her family's needs in the host country.

Whilst training in language and practical affairs is quite straightforward, cross-cultural training is not; it is complex and deals with deep-rooted behaviors. The actual process of cross-cultural training should result in the expatriate learning both content and skills that will improve interactions with host-country individuals by reducing misunderstandings and inappropriate behaviors. Black and Mendenhall suggest that trainers should apply social learning theory to this process by using the behavioral science techniques of incentives and rehearsal until the trainee internalizes the desired behaviors and reproduces them.

The result is a state of adjustment, representing the ability to effectively interact with host nationals. The objective of this training is to ease the adjustment to the new environment by reducing cultural shock, a state of disorientation and anxiety about not knowing how to behave in an unfamiliar culture. The cause of culture shock is the trauma people experience in new and different cultures, where they lose the familiar signs and cues that they had used to interact daily life and where they must learn to cope with a vast array of new cultural cues and expectations. The symptoms of culture shock range from mild irritation to a deep-seated psychological panic or crisis. The inability to work effectively, stress within the family, and hostility toward host nationals are the common dysfunctional results of culture shock, often leading to the manager giving up and going home.

It is important to recognize the stages of culture shock to understand what is happening. Culture shock usually progresses through four stages, as described by Oberg:-

1.   the honeymoon stage, when positive attitudes and expectations, excitement, and a tourist feeling prevail (which may last up to several weeks);
2.   Irritation and hostility, the crisis stage when cultural differences result in problems at work, at home, and in daily living. Expatriates and family members feel homesick and disoriented, looking out at everyone (many never get past this stage);
3.   gradual adjustment, a period of recovery in which the 'patient' gradually becomes able to understand and predict patterns of behavior, use the language, and deal with daily activities, and the family starts to accept their new life; and
4.   biculturalism, the stage in which the manager and family members grow to accept and appreciate local people and practices and are able to function effectively in two cultures. Most of them never get to the fourth stage, operating acceptably at the third stage, but those who do report that their assignment is positive and growth oriented.

Training Techniques

There are many training techniques available to assist overseas expatriates in the adjustment process. These techniques are classified by Tung as :-

1.   area studies, that is documentary programs about the country's geography, economics, socio-political history, and so forth;
2.   culture assimilators, which expose trainees to the kinds of situations they are likely to encounter that are critical to successful interactions;
3.   language training;
4.   sensitivity training; and
5.   field experiences – exposure to people from other cultures within the trainee's own country. Tung recommends using these training methods in a complementary fashion: the trainee has increasing levels of personal involvement as she or he progresses through each method. Documentary and interpersonal approaches have been found to be comparable, with the most effective intercultural training occurring when trainees become aware of the differences between their own culture and the one they are planning to enter.

Similarly categorizing training methods, Koren suggests specific techniques, including a field experience called the host-family surrogate, where the MNC pays for and places an expatriate family with a host family as part of an immersion and familiarization program. Exhibit 1-9 shows this and other training methods, some examples of the techniques used for each method, and the purpose of each.

Most training programs take place in the expatriate's own country prior to posting. Whilst this is certainly a convenience, the impact of host-country (or in country) programs can be far greater than those conducted at home because crucial skills, such as overcoming cultural differences in intercultural relationships, can actually be experienced during in-country training rather than simply discussed.

In fact, some MNCs are beginning to recognize that there is no substitute for on-the-job training (OJT) in the early stages of the careers of those managers they hope to develop into senior-level global managers. Colgate-Palmolive, whose overseas sales represent two-thirds of is $6 billion in yearly revenue is one company whose management development programs adhere to this philosophy.

After training at headquarters, Colgate employees become associate product managers in the United States or abroad, and, according to John R. Garrison, manager of recruitment and development at Colgate, they must earn their stripes by being prepared to country-hop every few years. In fact, says Garrison, "That's the definition of a global manager: one who has seen several environments first hand." Exhibit 1-10 shows some other global management development programs for junior employees.

Training Host-Country Nationals

The continuous training and development of HCNs and TCNs for management positions is also important to the long-term success of multinational corporations. As part of a long-term staffing policy for a subsidiary, the ongoing development of HCNs will assist the transition to an indigenization policy. Furthermore, multinational companies like to have well-trained managers with broad international experience available to take charge in many intercultural settings whether at home or abroad. Such managerial skills are increasingly needed in U.S. – Japanese joint ventures, a good example being G.M. Toyota in Freemont, California. There, managers as well as employees from both America and Japan learn to work side by side and adjust to a unique blend of country and corporate culture. For the Americans in this organization, helping to acculturate the Japanese employees not only demonstrates friendly goodwill but is a necessary part of securing their own future in the company.

In another common scenario also requiring the management of a mixture of executives and employees, American and European MNCs presently employ Asians as well as Arab locals in their plants and offices in Saudi Arabia, bringing together three cultures; well-educated Asian managers living in a Middle Eastern, highly traditionally society and employed by a firm reflecting Western technology and culture. This kind of situation involves the integration of multiple sets of cultural based values, expectations, and work habits.

Exhibit 1-7

Categories of Relations Expatriate Managers Must Maintain

Home Country   Host Country

Headquarters   External   Relations with
Relations   Relations   Home Government

                                     Expatriate
                                     Manager

Relations   Family   Internal
With Host   Relations   Relations
Government

A Model For Developing Key Expatriate Executives

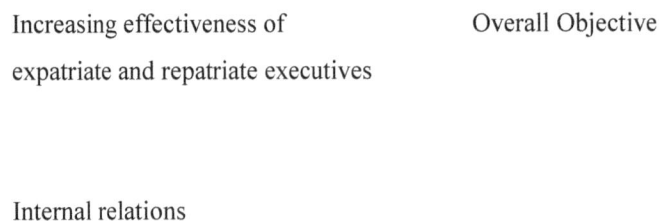

Exhibit 1-8

A Model For Developing Key Expatriate Executives

        Increasing effectiveness of   Overall Objective
        expatriate and repatriate executives

        Internal relations

Feedback	External relations Family relations Relations with host government Headquarters relations Relations with home government	Problem Recognition
Feedback	Review terms and conditions of assignment Increase cultural awareness Increase knowledge of host country Impart working knowledge of the foreign language Increase conflict management skills Minimize re-entry problems	Development Objectives
Feedback	How much development ?	Assessment of Development Needs
Feedback	Pre-departure training Orientation Area study Language instruction Cross-cultural T-group Behavioral stimulation Case method Post-arrival training Orientation and training Inter-group problem solving Re-entry training	Development Methods
Feedback	Knowledge about cultural, political, Economic, business, legal, and social Factors of the host country Awareness of the needs and expectations of the different parties interested in international operation Awareness of the problems of family relations in the Host country	Intermediate Result

| Evaluation | Effectiveness of the expatriate Executives | Desired Result |

| Feedback | Re-entry training | Development Methods |

| Evaluation | Effectiveness of the repatriate Executives | Desired Result |

Exhibit 1-9

Training Techniques For Expatriate Preparation

Method	Techniques	Purpose
Didactic- Informational Training	* lectures * Reading material * Videotapes * Movies	Area studies, company operations parent-country institutions
Intercultural Experiential Workshops Sensitivity Training	* Cultural assimilators * Simulations * Role playing * communication Workshops * T groups * Outward Bound trips	Culture-general, culture-specific negotiations skills; reduce ethnocentrism Self-awareness, communication style, empathy, listening skills, nonjudgementalism
Field Experiences	* Meeting with ex-PCNs * Minicultures * Host-family surrogate	Customs, Values, beliefs, nonverbal behavior, religion
Language Skills	* Classes * Cassettes	Interpersonal communication job requirement, survival necessities.

Exhibit 1-10

Developing Global Managers

- 113 -

Company	Program
American Express Co's Travel-related services unit	Gives American business-school students summer jobs in which they work outside the U.S. for up to 10 weeks. Also transfers junior managers with at least two years experience to other countries.
Colgate-Palmolive Co	Trains about 15 recent college graduates each year for 15 to 24 months prior to multiple overseas job stints.
General Electric Co's Aircraft-engine unit	Will expose selected midlevel engineers and managers to foreign language and cross-cultural training even though not all will live abroad.
Honda of Americas Manufacturing Inc.	Has sent about 42 U.S. supervisors and managers to the parent company in Tokyo for up to three years. After preparing them with six months of Japanese language lessons, cultural training and lifestyle orientation during work hours.
Pepsi Inc's International Beverage division	Brings about 25 young foreign managers a year to the U.S. for one year assignments in bottling plants.
Raychem Corp.	Assigns relatively inexperienced Asian employees (from clerks through middle managers) to the U.S. for six months to two years.

Chapter Five

Managing People : The Leadership Dimension

Fundamentals of Leadership

Leadership is the process of influencing people to direct their efforts toward the achievement of some particular goal or goals. When one realizes that much of history, political science, and the behavioral science are either directly or indirectly concerned with leadership, the statement that more concern and research has focused on leadership than on any other topic becomes believable. With all this attention over the years, however, there still is no generally agreed on definition, let alone firm answers to which approach is more effective than others in the international arena. Leadership is vastly recognized as being very important in the study of international management, but relatively little effort has gone to systematically studying and comparing leadership approaches throughout the world. Most international research efforts on leadership have been directed toward a specific country or geographic area.

Two comparative areas provide a foundation for understanding leadership in the international arena:

1.   the philosophic grounding of how leaders view their subordinates; and
2.   Leadership approaches as reflected through use of autocratic participative characteristics and behaviors of leaders. The philosophies and approaches used in the United States usually are quite different from those employed by leaders in overseas organizations, although these differences often are not as pronounced as is commonly believed.

Leadership Behaviors and Styles

Leader behaviors can be categorized into three broad recognized styles:

1.   authoritarian;
2.   paternalistic; and
3.   participative

Authoritarian Leadership

This leadership styles make use of work-centered behavior that is designed to ensure task accomplishment. As illustrated in Figure 1-23, this leader behavior typically involves the use of one-way communication from manager to subordinate. The focus of attention usually is on work progress, work procedures, and road blocks that are preventing goal attainment. Although this leadership style often is effective in handling crises, some leaders employ it as their primary style regardless of the situation.

Paternalistic Leadership

These leadership styles make use of work-centered behavior coupled with a protective employee-centered concern. This leadership style can be best summarized by the statement, "work hard and the company will take care of you." This approach was described in Geert Hofstede, "The cultural Relativity of organizational practices and Theories; and perhaps is best supported by cultures such as those found in Japan. Paternalistic leaders expect everyone to work hard, in turn, the employees will be guaranteed employment and given security benefits such as medical and retirement programs. Paternalistic leaders often are referred to as "soft" side of Theory X of Mcgreggor's Theorem on motivation, this theory X leaders because of their strong emphasis on strictly controlling their employees coupled with concern for their welfare. They usually adopt a pedagogical approach to their employees as strict but caring parents as would to their children.

One method of comparing and contrasting authoritative and paternalistic leaders is in terms of Likert's management systems or leadership styles, as shown in Table 1-11. As illustrated, an authoritarian leader is characterized by Likert's system 1, and a paternalistic leader is characterized by system 2.

Participative Leadership

This type of leadership style make use of both a work-centered and people-centered approach. Participative leaders typically encourage their people to play an active role in assuming control of their work, and authority commonly is highly decentralized. In relation to Likert's four systems shown in Table 1-11, participative leaders are characterized by sytem 3. (Likert's system 4 leaders are fully democratic and go beyond the participative style). Another way of characterizing participative leaders is in terms of the managerial grid, which is a traditional, well-known method of identifying leadership style. As shown in Figure 1-24, participative leaders are on the 9, 9 position of the grid. This is in contrast to paternalistic leaders, who tend to be about 9,5 and autocratic leaders, who are more of a 9,1 position on the grid. Participative leadership is very popular in many technologically advanced countries. Such leadership has been widely espoused in the United States, England, and other Anglo countries, and it currently is very popular in Scandinavian countries as well. For example, at General Electric, managers are encouraged to use a participative style that delivers on commitment and shares the values of the firm, which is an approach that also is common in these other nations.

Figure 1-23

Leadership – Subordinate Interactions

Authoritarian Leader

Subordinate   Subordinate   Subordinate

One-way downward flow of information and influence from authoritarian leader to subordinates

Paternalistic Leader

Subordinate   Subordinate   Subordinate

Continual interaction and exchange of information and influence between leader and subordinates.

Participative Leader

Subordinate   Subordinate   Subordinate

Continual interaction and exchange of information and influence between leader and subordinates.

Table 1-11

Likert's Systems or Styles of Leadership

Leadership	System 1	System 2	System 3	System 4
Characteristic Leadership process used (extent to which superiors have confidence and trust in subordinates)	(Exploitive Autocratic) Have no confidence and trust in subordinates	(Benevolent Autocratic) Have con-descending confidence and trust, such as Master has in servant	(Participative) Substantial but not complete confidence and trust, still wish to keep control of decisions	(Democratic) Complete confidence and trust in all matters
Character of motivational forces (underlying motives tapped)	Physical Security, economic needs, and Some use of the desire for status	Economic needs and moderate use of ego motive (eg desire for status, affiliation, And Achievement)	Economic needs and considerable use of ego and other major motives (eg, desire for new experiences)	Full use of economics ego, and other major motives such as motivational forces arising from group goals.
Character of communication process (amount of interaction and communication aimed at achieving organization's objectives).	Very Little	Little	Quite a bit	Much, with both individuals and groups.
Character of interaction influence process (amount and character of interaction)	Little inter-action and always with fear and distrust	Little inter-action and usually with same con-descension by	Moderate inter-action, often with fair amount of confidence	Extensive friendly interaction with high degree of confidence and trust.

		Superiors; fear and caution by subordinates	and trust	
Character of Decision-making process (at what level in organization are decisions formally made)	Bulk of decisions at top of organization	Policy at top: many decisions with prescribed frame work made at lower levels but usually checked with top before action is taken	Broad policy decision at top; more specific decisions of lower levels	Decision making widely done throughout organization although well integrated through linking process provided by overlapping group
Character of goal setting or ordering (manner in which usually done)	Orders issued	Orders issued, opportunity to comment may exist	Goals are set or orders issued after discussion with subordinates of problems and planned action	Except in emergencies, goals are usually established by group participation

Figure 1-24

The Managerial Grid

High	9	1-9	Management Style Thoughtful attention to needs of people for satisfying relationships leads to a comfortable friendly organization atmosphere and work tempo	9.9	Management Style Work accomplished is from committed people; interdependence through a "common stake" in organization purpose leads to relationships of trust and respect
	8				
Con- cern	7				
for	6				
people/ relation- ship	5		5.5 Management Style Adequate organization performance is possible through balancing the necessity to get out work with maintaining morale of people at a satisfactory level		
	4				
	3				
	2	1.1	Management Style Exertion of minimum effort to get required work done is appropriate to sustain organization membership	9.1	Management Style Efficiency in operation results from arranging conditions of work in such a way that human element interface to a minimum degree
	1				
	0	1	2 3 4 5 6	7 8 9	

Concern for Production Task

- 119 -

Differences between Japanese and U.S. Leadership Styles

In a number of ways, Japanese leadership styles differ from those in the United States. For example, the Haire and Associates study found that except for internal control, large U.S. firms tend to be more democratic than small ones, whereas in Japan, the profile is quite different. A second difference is that younger U.S. mangers appear to express more democratic attitudes than their older counterparts on all four leadership dimensions, but younger Japanese fall into this category only for sharing information and objectives and in the use of internal control. Simply put, evidence points to some similarities between U.S. and Japanese leadership styles, but major differences also exist.

A number of reasons have been cited for these differences. One of the most common is that Japanese and U.S. managers have a fundamentally different philosophy of managing people. Table 1-12 provides a comparison of seven key characteristics that come from the work of William Ouchi, author of the widely recognized Theory Z, which combines Japanese and U.S. assumptions and approaches. Note in the table, that the Japanese leadership approach is heavily group-oriented, paternalistic, and concerned with the employee's work and personal life. The U.S. leadership approach is almost the opposite.

Another difference between Japanese and U.S .leadership styles is how senior-level managers process information and learn. Japanese executives are taught and tend to use variety amplification, which is the creation of uncertainty and the analysis of many alternatives regarding future action. By contrasting, U.S. executives are taught and tend to use variety reduction ,which is the limiting of uncertainty and the focusing of action on a limited number of alternatives. As shown in Table 1-13 are some specific characteristics of these two approaches.

In this study of processing information and learning examined the leadership styles used by Japanese and U.S. senior managers, it is found that the Japanese focused very heavily on problems while the U.S. managers focused on opportunities. The Japanese were more willing to permit poor performance to continue for a time so that those who were involved would learn from their mistakes, but the Americans worked to stop poor performance as quickly as possible. Finally, the Japanese sought creative approaches to managing projects and tried to avail relying on experience, but the Americans sought to build on their experiences.

There is another major reason accounting for differences in leadership styles is that the Japanese tend to be more ethnocentric than their U.S. counterparts. The Japanese think of themselves as Japanese managers who are operating overseas, most do not view themselves as international managers. As a result, even if they do adapt their leadership approach on the surface to that of the country in which they are operating, they still believe in the Japanese way of doing things and are reluctant to abandon it.

Table 1-12

Japanese vs U.S. Leadership Styles

	Philosophical Dimension	Japanese Approach	U.S. Approach
1.	Employment	Often for life; layoffs are rare	Usually short-term; layoffs are common
2.	Evaluation and promotion	Very slow; big promotions may not come for the first 10 years	Very Fast; those not quickly promoted often seek employment elsewhere

3.	Career Paths	Very general; people rotate from one area to another and become familiar with all areas of operations	Very specialized: people tend to stay in one area (accounting, sales, etc) for their entire careers
4.	Decision making	Carried out via group decision making	Carried out by the individual manager
5.	Control mechanism	Very implicit and informed people rely heavily on trust and goodwill	Very explicit, people know exactly what to control and how to do it.
6.	Responsibility	Shared collectively	Assigned to individuals
7.	Concern for Employees	Management's concern extends to the whole life, Business and social of the worker	Management concern basically with the individual's work life only.

Table 1-13

Japanese and U.S. Senior Management Approaches To Processing Information

Japanese Senior Management	U.S. Senior Managment
Approach (Variety Amplification)	Approach (Variety Reduction)
State a policy that ALL phenomena are relevant	State a policy that focuses only on reluctant issues and sources of information

Require all employees to be identifiers of corporate problems and opportunities	Identify specific employees who will identify problems and opportunities
Seek a large quantity of information from the environment	Seek only high quality information from the environment
State a desire for the firm to attain an idea, a dream	State a desire for the firm to attain a realistic level, a goal
Focus on creating challenges, barriers to hurdle and problems to solve	Focus on taking advantage of opportunities, holes in the barrier to crawl through
Vitalize people	Direct people

Universalism in Leadership

The question of universality of leadership behavior had been on the minds of many researchers in this field. Do effective leaders, regardless of their country culture or job, act similarly? A second, and somewhat linked; research inquiry has focused on the question: Are there a host of specific behaviors, attitudes, and values that leaders in the twenty-first century will need in order to be successful? So far, the findings have been mixed. Some researchers have found that there is a trend toward universalism for leadership; others have concluded that culture continues to be a determining factor and an effective leader, for example, in Sweden will not be as effective in Italy if he or she employs the same approach. One of the most interesting researches has been conducted recently by Bass and his associate and has focused on the universality and effectiveness of both transformation and transactional leadership.

Transformational and Transactional Leadership

Transformational leaders are visionary agents with a sense of mission who are capable of motivating their followers to accept new goals and new ways of doing things. Transactional leaders are individuals who exchange rewards for effort and performance and work on a "something for something" basis. Do these types of leaders exist worldwide and is their effectiveness consistent in terms of performance? Bass, drawing on the analysis of studies conducted in Canada, India, Italy, Japan, New Zealand, Singapore and Sweden, as well as the United States, discovered that very little of the variance in leadership behavior could be attributed to culture. In fact, in many cases he found that national differences accounted for less than 10 percent of the results. This led him to create a model of leadership and conclude that "although this model.......may require adjustments and fine-tuning as we move across cultures, particularly into non-Western cultures, overall, it holds up as having considerable universal potential.

Simply put, Bass discovered that there was far more universalism in leadership than had been believed previously. Additionally, after studying thousands of international cases, he found that the most effective managers were transformational leaders and they were characterized by four interrelated factors. For convenience, the factors are referred to as the "4 Is" and they can be described this way:

1. Idealized influence – Transformational leaders are a source of charisma and enjoy the admiration of their followers. They enhance pride, loyalty, and confidence in their people and they align these followers by providing a common purpose or vision, mission, and beliefs in clear-cut ways, thus providing an easy-to-understand sense of purpose regarding what needs to be done.
2. Inspiration motivation. These leaders are extremely effective in articulating their vision, mission, and beliefs and clear-cut ways, thus providing an easy-to-understand sense of purpose regarding what needs to be done.
3. Intellectual stimulation. Transformation leaders are able to get their followers to question old paradigms and to accept new views of the world regarding how things now need to be done.
4. Individualized consideration. These leaders are able to diagnose and elevate the needs of each of their followers through individualized consideration, thus furthering the development of these people.

Bass also discovered that there were four other types of leaders. All of these were less effective than the transformational leader, although the degree of their effectiveness (or ineffectiveness) still varies. The most effective of the remaining four types was labeled the contingent reward (CR) leader by Bass. This leader classifies what needs to be done and provides both psychic and material rewards to those who comply with his or her directives. The following most effective manager is the active management-by-exception (MBE-A) leader. This individual monitors follower performance and takes corrective action when deviations from standards occur. The third type of manager, in terms of effectiveness is the passive management-by-exception (MBE-P) leader. This leader takes action or intervenes in situations only when standards are not met. And finally, there is the Laissez-faire (LF) leader. This manager avoids intervening or accepting responsibility for follower actions.

Bass found that through the use of higher-order factor analysis it is possible to develop a leadership model that illustrates the effectiveness of all five types of leaders: Its (transformational), CR, MBE-A, MBE-P, and Figure 1-25 presents this model. The higher the box in the figure and the further to right on the shaded base area, the more effective and active the leader. Note that the 4 I's box is taller than any of the others in the figure and it is located more to the right than any of the others. The CR box is second tallest and second closest to the right, on down to the LF box which is the shortest and furthest from the right margin. Bass also found that the 4 I's were positively correlated with each other, but less so with contingent reward. Note also, there was a near zero correlation between the 4 I" and management-by-exception styles, and there was an inverse correlation between these four factors and the laissez-faire leadership style.

Does this mean that effective leader behaviors are the same regardless of country? Bass has concluded that this statement is not quite true, but there is far more universalism than people have believed previously. In organizing his findings in perspective, he has concluded that there certainly would be differences in leadership behavior from country to country. For example, he has noted that transformational leaders in Honduras would have to be more directive than their counterparts in Norway. Moreover, culture can create some problems in using universal leadership concepts in countries such as Japan, where the use of contingent reward systems is not as widely used as in the West. Where there is a great belief that things will happen "if God wills" and not because a leader has decided to carry them out. Yet, even, after taking these differences into consideration, Bass contends that universal leadership behavior is far more common than many people realized.

Figure 1-25

An Optimal Profile Of Universal Leadership Behaviors

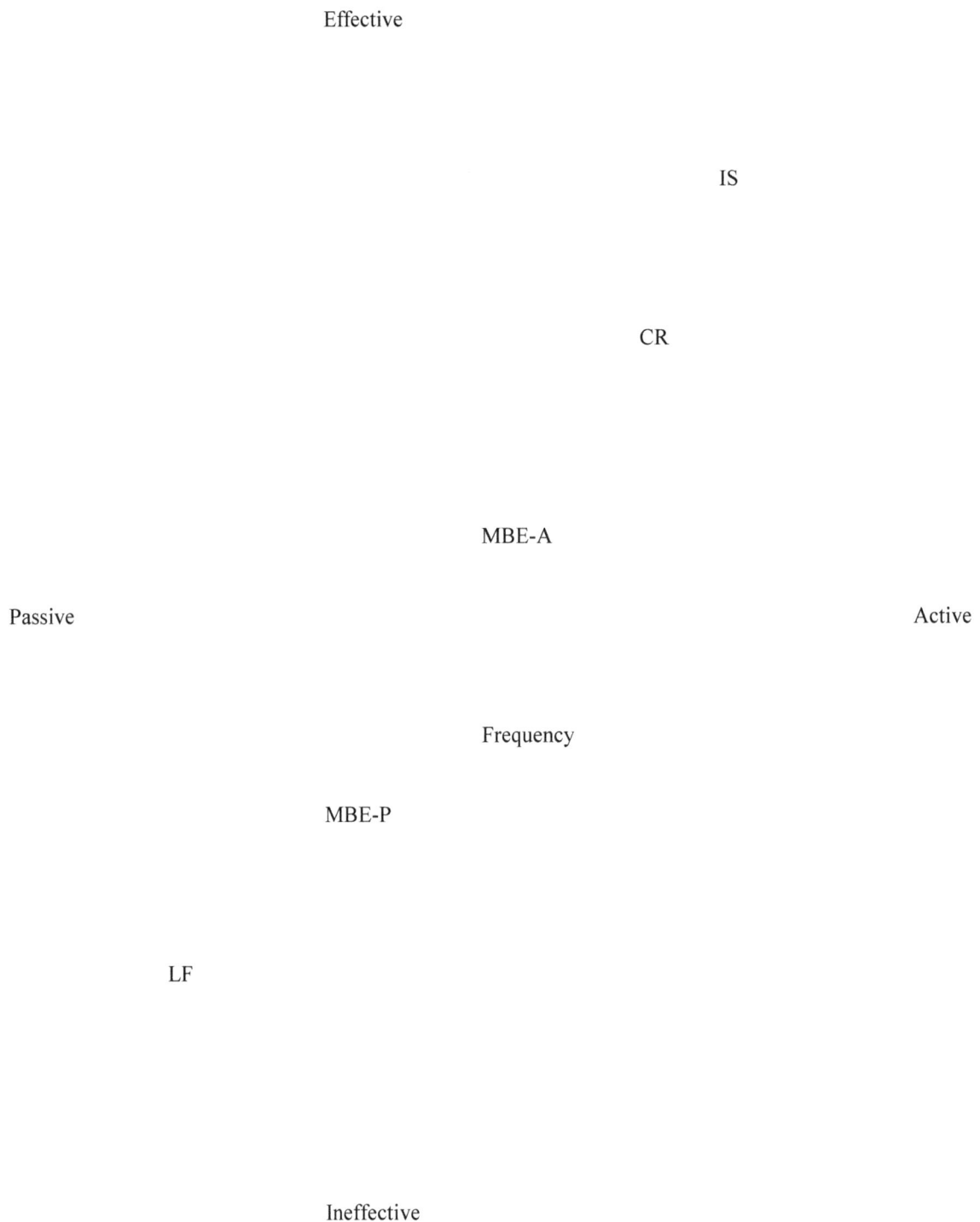

Effective

IS

CR

MBE-A

Passive   Active

Frequency

MBE-P

LF

Ineffective

Motivating People : The Challenge of Cultural Diversity

The fact that people and societies differ, international managers must adapt to unusual circumstances and become culturally sensitive to differences in foreign work environments. In no instance is this requirement more important than when managers are challenged to motivate foreign employees. They can rely on no universal rules to accomplish this goal. That statement does not mean that well-founded concepts of motivation contribute nothing, only that the principles of motivation theories cannot be generalized to all cultures. Managers must find the methods that work best within their own environments and with their particular employees. Research about motivation in the international context has revealed interesting contrasts.

In order to motivate effectively, International Managers need to know how to reduce the confusion about motivating people in other cultures and subsequently to suggest broad guidelines that may help them to understand their own situations. This chapter does not attempt to assess the inability of motivation theories per se; researchers have left much confusion on this score to allow productive argument here. However, the chapter will briefly review the foremost theories, and make discussion on fundamental concepts. The theories will be discussed in relation to human values and how people from different parts of the world seek fulfillment at work. For example, an understanding of differences in human values among the world's societies is crucial to a further understanding of why people from one nation earnestly pursue monetary gains, yet people elsewhere do not have much regard for wage incentives. In other cases, workers who put high value on group harmony will criticize coworkers who want to achieve individual recognition. The concepts and methods of work and a job evoke different meanings among people from other cultures, and therefore if incentives to will differ.

Motivation in the Cross-Cultural Context

In broad terms, motivation is the stimulus that drives behavior. It consists of all the forces that cause people to behave in certain ways, including forces from within the individual, from other people who can influence behavior and from within the surroundings. Figure 1-26 illustrates a process in which these three sources of motivation combine in the first stage to activate behavior, then are coupled to performance, and eventually become linked to perceived rewards. Motivational factors at the heart of this model can be examined individually, however, they are not mutually exclusive influences.

The first characteristic emphasizes the origination of motivation within a person, creating a capability for generating one's own momentum for working or taking initiative. The second characteristic implies that motivation is influenced by other people, in occupational situations, it is influenced by external stimuli such as pay, promotion opportunities, supervision praise, threats, potential ridicule, and disciplinary action. If a manager could identify cause and effect relationships between each of these variables and how well individuals work, then motivating people would be a relatively easy task, but caused effects cannot be reliably determined.

This is definitely evident in an evaluation of the third characteristic, called situational factors. Individual behavior is influenced by the work environment, which includes influences from society, close associates, technology that defines what people do and how they work, leadership behavior, and circumstance that arise in the process of working.

A manager can easily identify these three forces at work every day, although many people never become consciously aware of them. For example, a teenager with decent moral values may not be tempted to shoplift, yet the same person roaming through a store with a group of youngsters may become a shoplifter. Obviously, a teenager who might shoplift on his or her own accord may be prevented from doing so merely through a belief that group members would not approve of such behavior. Work behavior is subject to the same type of influence, exerted through social or cultural expectations, peer pressure, or personal values. Individuals subconsciously evaluate their circumstances and then act, speak, dress, work, and play in way, that they perceive to be congruent with their environments.

These three characteristics of motivation become much more complicated in an international context. International managers may have very little understanding of foreign cultures or social systems, and they are often clueless about deeply embedded individual values. The international manager's job would be much easier if values were universal, but these values differ substantially among the world's societies. Simply put, people are not motivated by the same rewards in different societies. They do not have similar expectations for pay, promotion, or personal recognition. Workers in one society may respond well to certain types of incentives that are repulsive elsewhere. As people have different expectations about their jobs and careers. Their work related behaviors differs form one society to the next, and, in each society, employers expect different rewards for their efforts. Work related values are not universal but instead reflect patterns of behavior embedded in each culture.

No doubt, researchers are looking for common bonds across cultures have found some evidence to suggest that motivation can be modeled along international lines. Before exploring these principles, it is important to establish several preliminary observations. First, motivation theories have evolved primarily in the United States, and consequently they represent a western or U.S. based perspective. Contrasting among Asian, Middle Eastern, African, Latin American, and even many European societies reveal anomalies in the fundamental assumptions on which the leading theories are based. Second, research has failed to show that motivation theories can be consistently generalized, even within specific societies; attempts to validate them have not escaped controversy. Third, none of the theories have resulted in clear recommendations that managers can reliably employ on a broad scale. With these caveats in mind, this study reviews the contributions of each theory to the current understanding of what people expect from their labors and what motivates them to do effective work.

Motivation in a Culturally Diverse Organization

Global organizations, by definition, are actually diverse organizations that require executive coordination of practices that accommodates a variety of perspective from many different people. Addressing diversity is, therefore, an important dimension of international management. Within a business unit, diversity compels attention for the human dimensions of managing small teams and personal relationships. The conceptual framework for managing a globally diverse workforce is not significantly different from that for addressing business unit diversity issues, but the range of issues spaces more complicated variations in a globally integrated firm.

Diversity encapsulates differences in human characteristics that arise from national origin, gender, race, ethnicity, religion, language, age, socioeconomic statues, and cultural values. Sensitive distinctions also arise due to differences in marital status, sexual orientation, physical abilities, and political ideologies. Perhaps the list does not end here. Clearly, any definitive prescription for managing a workforce with substantial variations in these characteristics would pose a complex challenge.

International managers can approach the topic in three ways. First, from a domestic perspective, they must allow for changing demographics, immigration, and employment practices that influence diversity in their home-country organizations. Second, managers must evaluate their responsibilities in foreign subsidiaries, where patterns of expatriation introduce new and diverse individuals and where local workforce displays diversity judged by internal standards, despite the appearance of homogeneity to outsiders. Third, diversity affects management of home-country employees by domestic managers reporting to foreign owners.

Managerial Challenge

Foreign firms tend to mix expatriates and local managers for their U.S. subsidiaries. In particular, European firms prefer to fill key positions with their own people. Though American executives sometimes work in European subsidiaries, it is a relatively uncommon phenomenon, very few American managers actually want to work for European firms, because they can seldom envision more than limited careers. The same argument can be made for natives of almost any European host country considering employment with U.S. or other foreign firms, but Japanese companies have this preference for home-country talent to extremes.

Very rarely do Japanese firms recruit host-country executives for their U.S. or European operations, and those have been hired have only recently taken their positions. Japanese companies have strong preference to staff their entire senior management cadres by Japanese nationals. For example, Matsushita assigns more than 700 senior managers to foreign posts at any one time, many of them in the United States. This known fact causes serious problems for domestic recruitment of both managers and employees. U.S. workers experience serious difficulties working under Japanese managers, beginning with language and cultural constraints. Given their choice, most would rather work for U.S. companies where they understand the reward systems and career opportunities.

Cultural Challenge

The descriptions of U.S. culture, from exhaustive research efforts ranging from contrasts between Mexican and U.S. workers in Maquiladoras to Hofstede's decade of investigations, emphasize attitudes of independence. Americans easily tolerate ambiguity, job mobility, informality and self-determined careers. They prefer independence in work behavior and decision making. Europeans and Asians wonder at these characteristics. They prefer structure to relationships, predictability in careers, and broad acceptances of authority. Japanese managers usually experience problems in the United States in their relations with female employees; Japan's generally accepted masculine prerogatives do not travel well. The U.S. society also favors confrontation more than foreigners expect.

Japanese visitors perceive the United States as a dangerous environment, with its obvious conflicts among ethnic minority groups as well as prominent racial tension. All societies have their social ills, but the striking contrasts in the United States often create unusual challenges for managing diversity within the foreign-owned enterprise. Most of the difficulties arise from disparities in the cultural values of independence and personal freedom.

U.S. nationals going abroad encounter just as many difficulties, so they should not feel like their isolated nation stands against the world; indeed prevalent problems in the U.S. are comparable to those in many other countries.

A foreign firm operating in the United States must resolve the same issues of managing diversity as it would managing a domestic enterprise, but it faces more sensitive circumstances that results from obvious differences in foreign multinationals. The Japanese or Europeans must accept the heterogeneity in North America firms and pursue shared interests that transcend language, cultural, and organizational differences. Japanese firms for example, faces similar difficulties in their Latin American subsidiaries, and likewise the Europeans have gone through with similar problems in Japan.

Organizational Challenge

The cultural and managerial difficulties of foreign firms operating in the United States result in a chronic source of friction within multinational firms. U.S. multinational succeed abroad by integrating foreign subsidiaries into the U.S. model, however many instances reveal that individual U.S. nationals usually could not integrate well into foreign organizations. This difference suggests an uncomfortable hint of ethnocentricity, but it is also the result of the geographic dispersion of U.S. markets, where affiliates of foreign-owned parent organizations rely extensively on locally managed operations. Hence, tension results from disparities in expectations between U.S. managers and their foreign superiors. The emphasize and nurturing of an individual in high individualism country like U.S. tends to stifle hierarchical power as it sets up barriers against group-based activities. Workers may not, therefore, accept participative system that exists in much foreign organizations.

Figure 1-26

The Basic Motivation Process

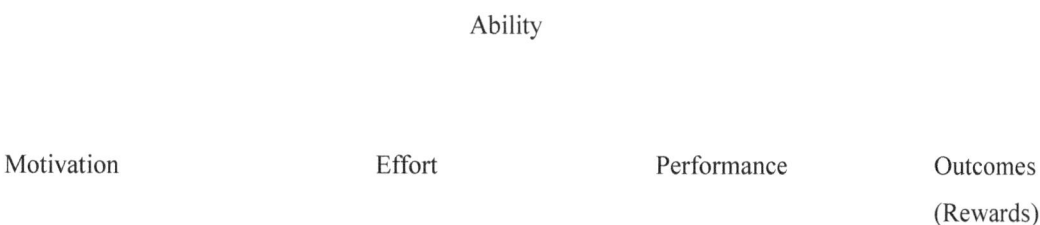

Ability

Motivation   Effort   Performance   Outcomes
                                                          (Rewards)

Motivation in Perspective

No standard set of principles for motivation can provide a prescription for managers either at home or abroad, and almost any recommendation, if given is either too trivial or too complex to permit practical implementation. However several guidelines can help managers to cultivate sensitivity to cross-cultural differences in motives. Also, certain measures may help to reduce conflicts that arise in diverse multicultural environments.

The first point to take note is that motivation can emerge from within an individual's own values or self-directed initiatives. Hence, success requires an understanding of how and why individuals behave as they do; this need imposes a perplexing responsibility on international mangers. Motivation also can result from external influences, organizational incentives, and leader member relationships. Because these motives vary with cultural values, locations, ethnic profiles, and many other factors, they are called situational variables. International managers should, therefore, avoid assumptions about motivation within their home cultures. Instead, they should reach for a deeper understanding of the expectations and customs that influence local behavior. It is this reason that motivation theories which favor a contingency approach often prove more effective than rigid theories. The variation in situational variables within a foreign subsidiary with a culturally diverse workforce require a continuous balancing process that challenges managers to consider individual motivational characteristics, patterns of cultural values, and situational variables that are the underlying factors of multicultural differences.

Secondly, understanding differences in the concepts of work and jobs throughout the world provides an equally important foundation for effective motivation. The motion of work takes on different meanings in Mexico, Germany, Russia, China, and the United States or Canada. Firms in different countries must accommodate underpinning beliefs in the value of work. They must also adapt to relationships with co-workers, superiors, and subordinates, and eventually seek to understand the priorities assigned to rewards received for work-related behavior in each environment.

International managers find their greatest personal rewards in success through new relationships with people from other cultures. They also experience their greatest frustrations in efforts to understand and adapt to expectations of their foreign colleagues and employees. This diversity creates psychological and sociological challenges that simply do not happen in a home culture, and these can range from perplexing problems to exciting opportunities.

Leadership in the Global Setting

The manager's quintessential responsibility is to help his people realize their own highest potential. Leadership is the process of influencing other people to behave in preferred ways to accomplish organizational objectives. In the business world, it is the management activity intended to optimize progress toward organizational objectives while also inspiring individual employees to fulfill their potential. Even though many researchers and philosophers have tried to explain how great men and women have persuaded people to follow them, scholars are still searching for an unambiguous explanation of leadership. One definition emphasizes a process of influencing behavior, a stimulating effect on group and individual performance. This concept is broad enough to be generally accepted almost anywhere in the world, but every culture puts a different dimension to the meaning of leadership.

Multicultural Leadership

Effective leadership involves the ability to inspire and influence the thinking, attitudes, and behavior of people. The importance of the leadership role cannot be overemphasized because the leader's interactions strongly influence the motivation and behavior of employees, and ultimately, the entire climate of the organization.

The multicultural leader tries to maximize leadership effectiveness by juggling several important, and sometimes conflicting, roles as:

1.   A representative of the parent firm,
2.   The manager of the local firm,
3.   A resident of the local community,
4.   A citizen of either the host country or of another country,
5.   A member of a profession, and
6.   A member of a family

Mason and Spich describe the leader's role as the interaction of two sets of variables, that is the content and the context of leadership. The content of leadership comprises the attributes of the leader and the decisions to be made, the context of leadership comprises all those variables related to the particular situation. The increased number of variables (political, economic and cultural) in the context of the managerial job abroad requires astute leadership. Some of the variables in the content and context of the leader's role in foreign settings are illustrated in Exhibit 1-11 (Factors Affecting Leadership Abroad). The multicultural leader's role thus blends leadership, communication, motivational, and other managerial skills within unique and ever-changing environments.

Exhibit 1-11

Factors Affecting Leadership Abroad

CONTENT

Attributes of the Person

Job position knowledge, experience,
and expectations
Longevity in company, country,
functional area.
Intelligence and cultural learning /
change ability.
Personality as demonstrated in values,
beliefs, attitudes toward foreign situations
Multiple memberships in work and
professional groups.
Decision and personal work style.

Characteristics of Decisions Situation

Degree of complexity, uncertainty, and risk
host-country information needs and
availability.
Articulation of assumptions and expectation
Scope and potential impact on performance
Nature of business partners
Authority and autonomy required
Required level of participation and
acceptance by employees, partners, and
government linkage to other decisions
Past management legacy
Openness to public scrutiny and
responsibility.

CONTEXT

Attributes of the Job / Position

Longevity and past success of former
Role occupants in the position
Technical requirements of the job
Relative authority / power
Physical location (eg, home office,
Field office).
Need for co-ordination, co-operation, and
integration with other units.
Resource availability
Foreign peer groups relations

Characteristics of the Firm and Business

Environment
Firm structure: size, location, technology,
tasks reporting, and communication patterns
Firm process : decision making, staffing,
control system, reward system, information
system, means of co-ordination, integration,
and conflict resolution.
Firm outputs : products, services, public
image, corporate culture, local history, and
community relations.
Business environment : social cultural,
Political-economic, and technological
aspects of a country/market.

Leadership Behaviors

Although, researchers in the United States have produced a substantial amount of literature on leader-subordinate behavior, in particular focusing on autocratic versus democratic leadership styles. Some similarity was found among such studies. Example will be McGregor, he proposes two extremes of leadership styles, based on the manager's assumptions about his or her employees. A Theory X manager exhibits autocratic behaviors, based on the assumption that people must be "made" to work and that their motivation is limited to satisfying safety and security needs. A Theory Y manager, in contrast, exhibits democratic behaviors, based on the assumption that people are motivated by the desire for achievement and responsibility.

Likewise, the Ohio State University leadership studies concluded that leadership behavior ranges from consideration, encouraging subordinates' participation and praising them, to initiating structure, emphasizing task performance and deadlines rather than the person.

Using an identical continuum, Blake and Mouton refer to "relations-oriented" compared to "task-oriented" leadership styles, using a grid to plot the styles of the managers they researched along this dimension. They recommend that maximal concern with both task and people (their "9-9" style) is usually ideal. Likert also describes leadership styles along a range from "exploitive autocratic" (system 1) to "democratic" (system 4).

It can, therefore be concluded that most research on American leadership styles describes managerial behaviors on, essentially, the same dimension, variously termed the autocratic versus democratic, the participative versus directive, the relations-oriented versus task-oriented, or the initiating structure versus consideration continuum. These studies were developed in the West, and conclusions regarding employee responses largely reflect the opinions of American workers. The democratic, or participative, leadership style has been recommended as the one more likely to have positive results with most American employees.

Contingency Leadership

The Culture Variable

Modern leadership theory recognizes that no single leadership style best suits all situations. Fiedler's contingency model thus poses that a leader should be well matched to a situation in the first place because leadership style is relatively inflexible. But, contrasting Fiedler's contingency model, House and Mitchell, in their path-goal theory, assumes that leaders can change their behavior to accommodate different situations. This theory, regarding leadership as proactive and constructive, proposes that the leader should clarify and facilitate the paths to goal attainment and then reward that attainment. The path-goal leadership model is based on the expectancy theory of motivation, which poses that a person's level of motivation depends on her or his perception of the likelihood of attaining various outcomes and the value she or he associate with those outcomes. Exhibit 1-12 illustrates the integrative model of the leadership process – pulling together the variables on culture, leadership, and motivation, showing the powerful contingency of culture as it affects the leadership role. The exhibit covers the broad environmental factors through to the outcomes affected by the entire leadership situation. As illustrated in the exhibit, the broad context where the manager operates requires adjustment in leadership style to all those variables relating to the work and task environment and the people involved. Cultural variables (values, work norms, the locus of control, and so forth), as they affect all the people involved, leader, subordinates, and work groups, then shape the content of the immediate leadership situation. The leader-follower interaction is then further shaped by the leader's choice of behaviors (autocratic, participative and so on) and the employee's attitudes toward the leader and the incentives. Motivation effects, various levels of effort, performance, and satisfaction results from these interactions, on an individual and a group level. These effects determine the outcomes for the company (productivity, quality) and for the employees (satisfaction, positive climate). The results and reward from those outcomes then act as feedback (positive or negative) into the cycle of the motivation and leadership process. Clearly, then, international managers should take seriously the culture contingency in their application of the contingency. Theory of leadership, meaning that they must adjust their leadership behaviors according to the context, norms, attitudes, and other variables in that society.

Transformational and Charismatic Leadership

Research on leadership in the United States has focused on the role of charismatic leadership and transformational leadership in revitalizing organizations. Such revitalization is considered particularly important to organizations trying to remain competitive in the international arena.

The term transformational leadership describes the process by which managers influence major changes in employees' attitudes and assumptions. This form of leadership aims to build commitment to achieve the organization's goals.

Another type of leadership, charismatic leadership, occurs when people have complete faith in their leader as a unique person, or superhero, following him or her with unquestioning acceptance and obedience. Similar to the trait theory, charismatic leadership theory focuses on the person as a leader, rather than on the leadership process. There has so far been little research on the cultural contingency of transformational or charismatic leadership; nevertheless, it is important to remain aware of new developments in leadership theory to consider their applicability around the world. Assumption can be made, for example that charismatic leadership would have a more powerful influence in Mexico, where managers are regarded as total people and father figures, then in the Untied States and much of Europe, where there is more separation between work roles and private lives. Likewise, transformational leadership would no doubt have more influence in collective societies, such as Japan, where there is a high level of identification and loyalty to the firm and its managers.

Exhibit 1-12

The Culture Contingency in the Leadership Process. An Integrative Model

Context	Content	Leader-follower Situation	Motivation Effects	Outcomes
External	Leader	Leader Behavior		
Origin	Cultural	Variables		
Political	Sensitivity	Autocratic or		
Economic	Values,	Participative		
Technological	Motives,	Task or people		
Cultural	Ability,	oriented		
	Experiences	Reward system		
	Source of	Transformational		
	Power			
	Personality,			
	Style			
Level of	Subordinates		Effort	Productivity
Divergence/	Values, norms		Performance	Quality
Convergence	Ability,	INTERACTION	Ability to	Achievement
Of culture/	Experience		Achieve goals	of individual
Management	Needs,		satisfaction	and group goals
	Motives	INFLUENCE	Turnover	Positive climate
	Locus of		Absenteeism	satisfaction
	Control		Quality	

Internal	Work groups	Employee	
Origin	Values, norms	Behavior	Feedback
Organization	Work goals	Variables	
Factors	Authority	Expectancy	
Task factors	system	Achievement	
Resource	Group	Value of	
Availability	Processes	rewards	
Systems		Responsiveness	
Processes		to leader	Rewards
		Behaviors	
		Group response	

Motivation

The Effective International Leader

The question that International managers should ask themselves is what makes an effective international leader. The determinant factor to effectiveness is whether the leader or manager has and applied the appropriate skills to address a given situation. The key cross cultural leadership skills needed, according to Bass, is social perpetual skills, interpersonal competence, effective intelligence, and efficient work habits.

Some important information about what managers around the world consider necessary for interpersonal competence is provided by a cross-cultural study of 1,000 managers in 13 countries, in this study, Bass and Burger found seven factors to be linked with interpersonal competence:

1. preferred awareness (willingness to be aware of others' feelings)
2. actual awareness (actual understanding of oneself and others)
3. submissiveness (to rules and authority)
4. reliance on others (in problem solving)
5. favoring of group decision making
6. concern for human relations
7. cooperative peer relations

The skills and other competence of the leader comprise only one variable of the leadership context. Other variables include the followers, the peers, the superiors, the task, and the task environment. International managers must evaluate themselves and the total leadership environment to manifest good leadership.

Issues in Cross-Cultural Leadership

Leadership in an intercultural setting, regardless of whether the management of a joint venture, a subsidiary abroad, or a diverse work group in the home country, poses many questions. The fundamental question is whether we can apply leadership theory and research results from one country to another. Researchers have considerable doubts about the translatability of the word leader across national and cultural boundaries. Political, economic, and social variables result in different conceptions of leadership and the relative acceptability of certain styles.

The issues of the generalizability of leadership styles has implications for whether we can expect managers to be effective in foreign countries. From research, we can conclude that some dimensions of leadership are universally relevant, while others are culturally contingent. For example, the autocratic style is prevalent in more traditional and less developed countries, the participative style is common in democratic societies and developed countries.

Exceeding such generalizations managers would conduct research and consult with others to develop an appropriate leadership style for each unique mix of context and content variables.

An underlying question facing researchers – implicit in the issues of the generalize ability and the transferability of leadership practices is whether convergence is occurring (the shifting of individual styles to become more similar to one another). With increasing internationalization, the industrialized societies of Europe, Japan, and the Anglo-American world are converging. Multinationals are a considerable force for the global convergence of many values.

As postulated by Webber, three major forces point toward further convergence. First, technology will have a homogenizing effect on disparate national cultures by making workers' technical skills are important than their social status. Second, the increasingly similar forms of education accommodate more uniform technology worldwide, which then promotes further uniformity in business techniques and eventually in economies and cultures. Third, a higher standard of living fosters the development of similar pragmatic societal values in diverse cultures, replacing powerful divergent values. Hofstede, in fact, notes on increase in individualism among the 50 countries he surveyed between 1968 and 1972.

Convergence means that the world will continue to become smaller, with ever-increasing interaction across the boundaries between companies, institutions, and people. Cross-cultural leaders are a potential vehicle for convergence, blending cultural beliefs and management practices. The amount and pace of convergence will vary according to the relative power of the opposing forces for divergence. These forces include such factors as a country's stage of development, its location and natural resources, and the relative cultural inertia, or resistance to change.

Evidence of convergence has been observed in Egypt, for example, where we see a molding of Arab, Turkish, Pharoanic, Levantine, and European cultures as a result of rapid industrialization. Egyptians' traditional attitude toward the future is reflected in the word inshallah, meaning 'if God wills'. This fundamental religious value underlies their low-key attitude toward work, relationships, and accomplishments and dominates leader-subordinate relations.

Similar observations of convergence are noted in a study of the Arabian Gulf region. This region has become a strategic importance to many Western business, primarily because of its oil reserves, and the influence of Western managerial, practices has been quite evident, fueled by the numerous expatriate mangers located there and by the Western training of many local mangers. Researchers discovered a growing tendency toward participative management, not a usual management technique in a traditional society. These changes indicate, the strong influence of external variables in this region.

As leadership entails constant interactions with others (employees, peers, superiors, outside contacts), cultural influences on this critical management function are very strong. Obviously, other potential variables are intricately involved in the international management context, particularly those of economics and politics. Effective leaders usually examine carefully the whole leadership context and develop a sensitivity to others' values and expectations regarding personal and group interactions, performance, and outcome before they act accordingly.

International Teams: The Emerging Management Challenge

The Contrasting Social Environments for Teamwork

Benefits of teamwork and workplace empowerment have been firmly entrenched in leadership theories for almost half a century. The founding premises of total quality management and organizational redesign emphasize team development. The underpinning assumption of productivity improvement asserts that self-directed teams far outrace individuals working separately in autocratic systems. In additional, a pre-dominate theme for discussions of effective multinational expansion highlights the value of cross-cultural teams led by managers capable of creating fully integrated networks of operation. These are profound points, yet organizations throughout the world have heeded them only reluctantly, creating relatively few team-based activities compared to traditional, hierarchical, and perhaps autocratic decision-making system.

Why do any firms hesitate to adopt pervasively team-oriented structures that carry out activities in self-directed work environments? Many of the answer seem to come from the resilience of cultural values and the reinforcement they provide for well-ingrained patterns of behavior in each society. Consequently, teamwork is an important part of organizational life, and teams do play significant and even necessary roles in both domestic and international management systems. Yet, they remain supplement elements of mainstream management methods. In different societies, business persons find important contrasts in these team-based activities.

Group Development and Team Processes

International managers should be ready and adaptive to the various culturally diverse teams; they cannot venture overseas with preset models of team behavior in mind and expect to find ready welcome for their ideas. A multinational company seeking to establish international teams with multicultural representation faces a complex initial problem of reconciling how members from different cultures will fit into a team environment. It is after resolving this problem can management consider how to approach team activities. Unfortunately, to-date there is no rules for formulating international teams. For example, an IBM Latin American team will likely behave more paternalistically than an IBM European team that reflects Western concepts of joint decision making. Meanwhile, IBM's Japanese team may be a highly involved consensus-building group, while IBM staff in Malaysia or Saudi Arabia may work within autocratic styles tempered with religious tenets. A top management team with representatives from each of these regions would be a truly multicultural body with extreme differences about what teamwork means and how decisions are made. Hence, development in each multicultural team setting requires a unique approach based on reason for forming the team, its responsibilities, and the cultural profile of its members. The process of team formation does reveal some similarities throughout the world. The following is a guideline shows a broad view of a general process.

Stages of Group Formation

Every international team endeavor develops through various stages. Analysts have summarized these stages into four stages, which is known in management discipline as forming, storming, norming, and performing. Figure 1-27 described the stages.

Stage 1 : Mutual Acceptance

As a team begins to form, members unfamiliar with one another begin to share information, test one another's opinions and values by discussing non-threatening topics, and try to understand one another's expectations of teamwork. Often, a company can facilitate this stage and help members to reach mutual acceptance of one another through simulation games and team-building exercises conducted by consultants.

Figure 1-27

The Four Stages Of Group Development

Stage 1	Stage 2	Stage 3	Stage 4
Forming	Storming	Norming	Performing
Members share information about one another, get acquainted, test one another for acceptable behavior in the group	Task environment evolves with initial communication; decision making on group activities evolves	Group creates a sense of cohesion, and individuals evolve into roles that lead toward motivated substantive work	Clear group goals emerge, and group behaviors shows self-correction and focus on goal-oriented performance
Uncertainty and Apprehension	Potential conflict and Hostility	Solidification and Reconciliation	Group Confidence and Maturity

- 134 -

This activity represents a crucial stage of development for a multicultural team, because it prepares members for the attitudinal problems, perceptual differences, and communication constraints they must reconcile. A group facilitator therefore can provide valuable help in getting the group moving on the right track. This stage is also called forming to emphasize that the team accomplishes little substantive work; instead, the process emphasized team behavior and mutual understanding of how members will work together.

Stage 2: Communication and Decision Making

Once members of the team have adjusted to one another, the group leader begins pushing the teams to develop a statement of its initial purpose and to formulate objectives. This process often defines the group's structure and role expectations within the team. A self-directed group may complete a long process at this stage of development, as the team members carry out self-evaluations, establish their own agendas, and reconcile team-based priorities with individual interests. The process itself is an important aspect of team development, but it can be stressful.

Multicultural groups are particularly vulnerable to differences in opinions, because effective communication requires significant adaptation of behavior. Those members who simply cannot adapt to the team behavior will leave and others will join. This is called storming, because the process emphasizes brainstorming techniques and open communications to foster the team cohesion required to tackle more challenging work.

Stage 3: Motivation and Productivity

Also known as norming, this stage begins as the group successfully resolves differences that become apparent in stage 2. Ideally, this accommodation process creates a sufficiently cohesive team to pursue consensus on decisions. Members feel motivated to work together toward objectives that they have developed as a team. The members have reached a state of normalcy in their relations that leaves them comfortable with the entire team process and eager to achieve new and creative results as a team.

At this stage, various goals were develop, the group finds synergy in achieving its goals that were set. If the team had not mix well enough to synergise in Stage 2, then the success of the team may not materialize.

Stage 4: Control and Organization

At this stage, an effective group demonstrates sufficient maturity to spontaneously adjust behavior to performance and team objectives. In comparison, an evolving team still requires adaptation to team activities. In fact, this level of activity is the work cycle of the team, and it is suitably called the stage of performing. The team has evolved to a point where members understand their roles and expectations, and they can respond to group efforts without stressful attempts to consciously fit themselves into teams' relationship. In mature self-managed teams, there is a closely knitted feeling of family atmosphere and everyone work together knowing each other capabilities and moves.

Homogenous groups often advance very quickly through the team development stages. Unlike diverse teams, they have few differences to resolve, card members already share a grounded cultural identity on which to build later consensus. A multicultural group may need months, or even years, to mature into a smoothly functioning stage 4 team. Many teams may not reach the optimal point of self-control and effective performance. Failure is nearly as prevalent as exceptional success among diverse teams, and team failure usually results from irreconcilable cultural differences among the members.

Chapter Six

Conclusion

It would be presumptuous to suggest what the most significant challenge is likely to be in the twenty-first century. There is no magical formula to explain what is to unfold for management, yet clear evidence suggests that the fundamental nature of management is rapidly changing to reflect the characteristics of transnational enterprises. International Management firms, similar to transnational organizations, will eventually breakthrough political or economic borders, giving birth to a culturally transcendent organizational system of International relational networks. The nature of organizations will therefore transform to reflect an electronic means of knowledge data base supported by global information exchanges. Transaction processes will no longer follow functional relationships and diagrams of traditional organizational structures will have little meaning, when international teams take place in the organizational structure. In place of these idiosyncrasies, the emphasis will be focus on integrated systems of activities. Management will be transformed from operating priorities of implementation to an entrepreneurial proclivity for change and innovation.

These rather ambiguous changes suggest a need for managers to prepare for chaos and from that chaos to create feasible new systems of global organizations. To be pragmatic, tomorrow's managers must anticipate entirely new career expectations and brace themselves psychologically to work in rapidly changing world enterprises. Organizations will become repositories of knowledge with integrated systems of team-based activities, and managers' careers will be defined according to their abilities to develop and organize International Teams in dynamic multicultural International environments

Appendix – I

About Author

Loke Chee Shong obtained his PhD. In Business Decision Management from Pacific National University Of Professional Studies, also earned a PhD. In Education and Management, and a Masters of Business Administration from The International University of U.S.A. Appointed an Overseas Professor of The International University. He has extensive experience in the field of General Management, Property Management, Project Management and International Management having worked in the Industry for more than 25 years. Dr. Loke also earned a Post Graduate Diploma in Business Administration in Finance from The University Of Leeds, UK, He also earned a Post Graduate Diploma in Entrepreneurship from The Society Of Business Practitioner UK, and is a Certified Professional Manager. He holds a Bachelor of Science,(Hons). in Business Management from The University Of Bradford. UK, and a Bachelor of Science,(Hons). in Accounting and Finance. He also holds a Diploma in Commercial Law and a Bachelor of Science in Engineering, majoring in Mechanical Engineering. A Professional Engineer in Computer Hardware Engineering.

Dr. Loke teaches in Business Management, Marketing, Strategic Management, Economics and Property Management at both Bachelors and Masters Level. Currently He supervises Doctoral Students in their Doctoral Research work. He has previously taught at Technology Management Centre Singapore, in Property Management, in the Masters of Property Program of Newcastle University, Australia.

He also taught International Business Management, in the Masters Of Business Administration Program from both the University Of Rutherford and University of Strafford, USA. At the System Computer Training Centre Singapore.

He also lectured in the Masters Of Business Administration Program of La Trobe University, Australia, and Bachelors Program of University Of Southern Queensland at Global Universities Alliance. He taught Human Resource Management and Business Law at The Westminster Unicampus.

He was Head of Business, at Auston Institute Of Management & Technology, also taught in Business Strategy for Bachelors Program Of Coventry University UK. He supervises Bachelor degree students from Upper Iowa University in their final year projects. He also taught in Asia Pacific Management Institute, KAPLAN in Bachelor degree Program from La Trobe University, Australia. He lectured in International Business Management at Boston International School.

Currently he lectures in Global Marketing and Accounting at Lincoln Business School, Property Management, Masters Of Property, at Technology Management Centre, and Building Services Engineering at Princeton edcademy, accredited by Heriot Watt University UK., Facilities and Real Estate Management at Universal School Of Professional Studies. Currently, He is both an Academic Lecturer and a Free Lance Consultant in Business Management and Education.

Dr. Loke is married to his wife, Shirley, he has a son, named Joshua and a daughter, named Joyce. He and his family currently resides in Singapore.

Appendix – II

Index

T

Appendix – III

Notes

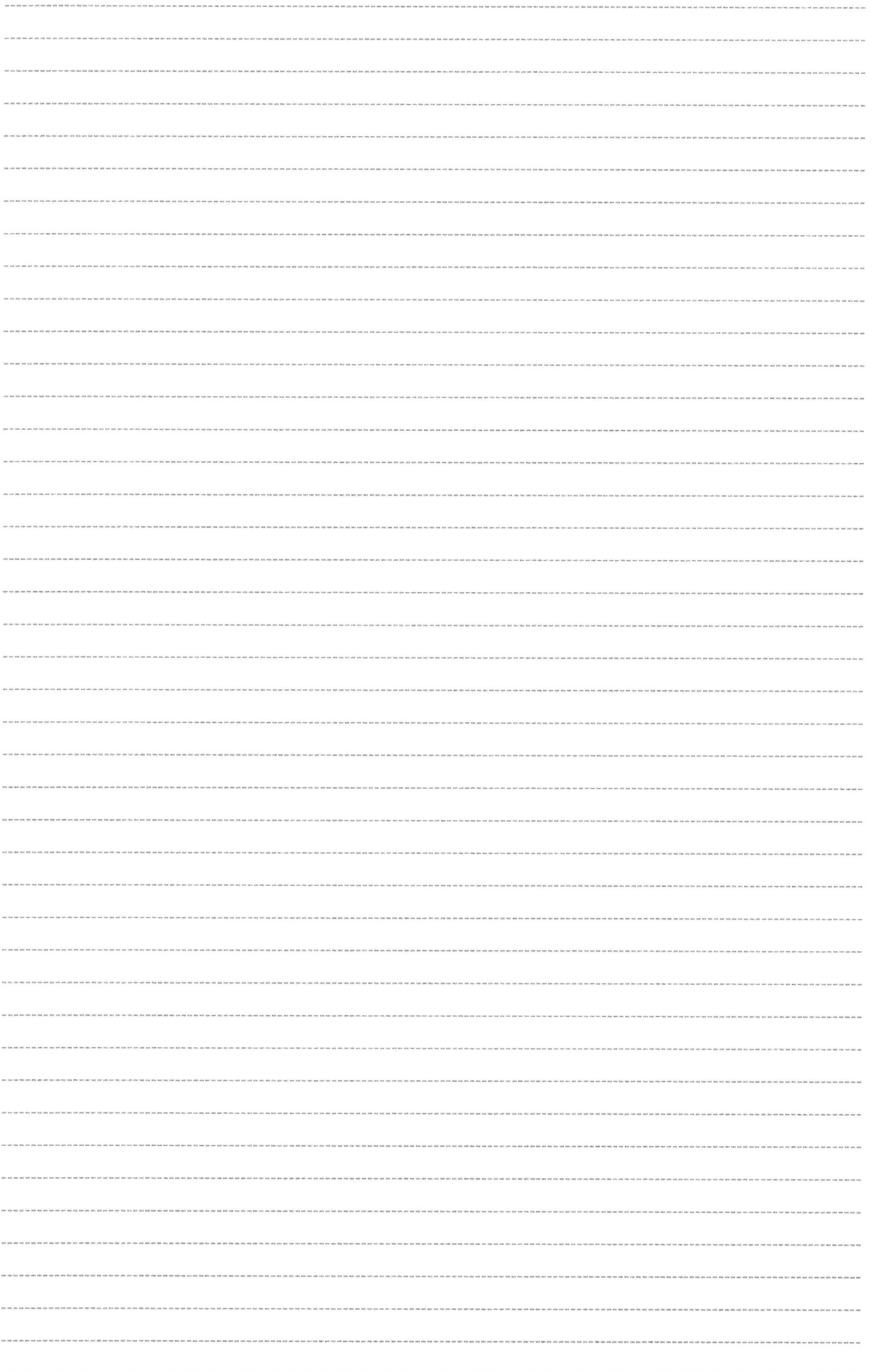

www.ingramcontent.com/pod-product-compliance
Lightning Source LLC
Chambersburg PA
CBHW080251200326
41519CB00023B/6955